**MAKE
WORLDS**

Jamaal Cox

# The power within

© 2021 **Europe Books** | London
www.europebooks.co.uk – info@europebooks.co.uk

ISBN 979-12-201-0713-6
First edition: April 2021

Distribution for the United Kingdom: **Vine House Distribution ltd**

Printed for Italy by Rotomail Italia
*Finito di stampare nel mese di aprile 2021*
*presso Rotomail Italia S.p.A. - Vignate (MI)*

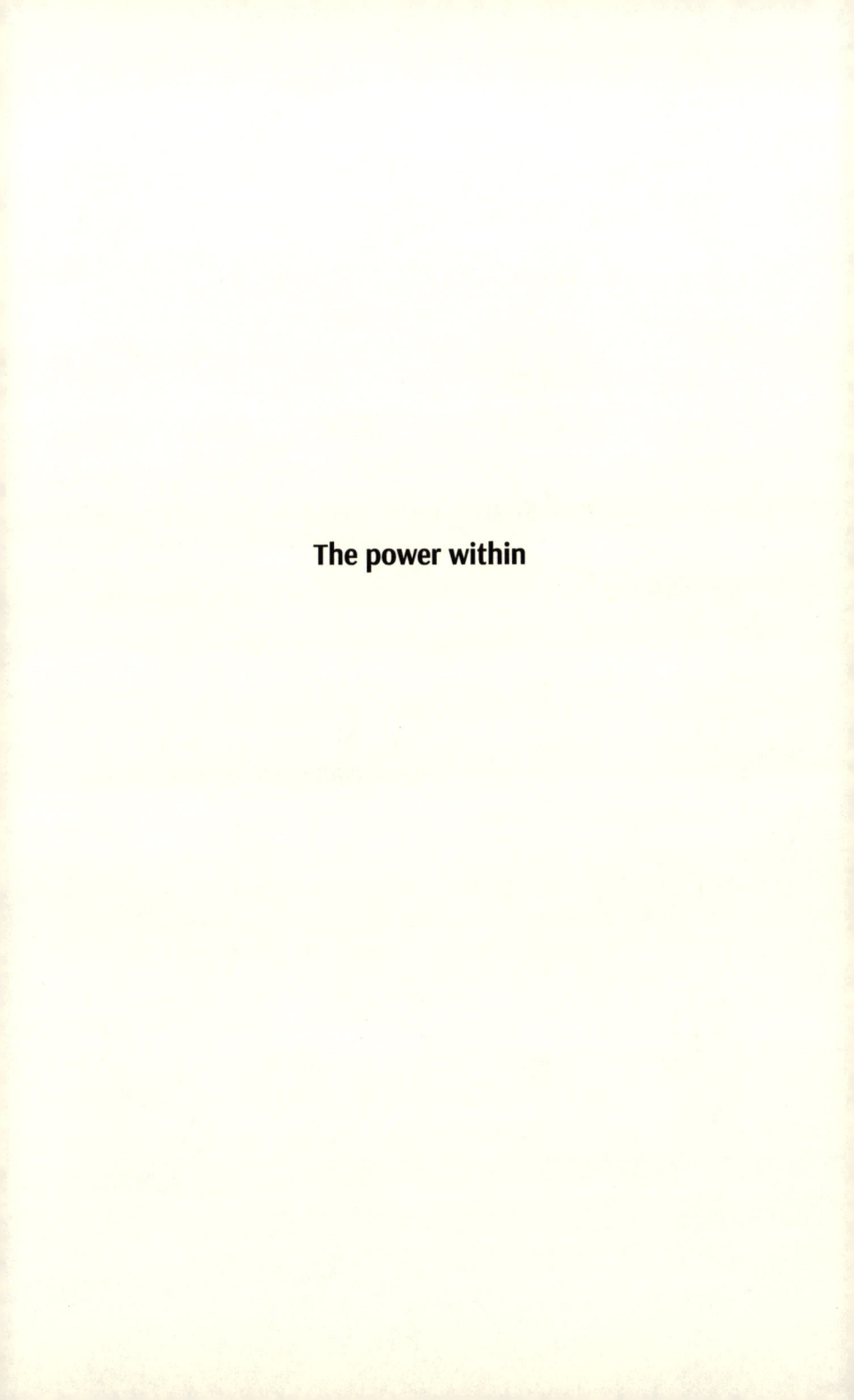

**The power within**

*To Spurgeon Cox:
Thank you, for it was your story that helped me
on this journey we call life.*

*I want to thank the publishers
for making this book possible.*

I want to acknowledge Rawan Hassan

*You are not weak for being too sensitive*
*To be sensitive is a beautiful thing*
*It takes strength to express your feelings*
*Continue to be who you are*
*Gentle like a bee*
*Like when a bee lands on a flower*
*Do not let people turn you into a wasp*
*Ready to sting and be angry at the world*
*Continue to be a bee*
*The world needs sensitive people like you*
*Just like a flower needs the bee.*

*Thank you, my love!*

The true story of Mr S G Cox.
You are the star of your show. You are the director and you are the producer. You decide whether your life is a hit or a flop.
When you get an idea, bring it to life.
Jamaal Cox

# INTRODUCTION

"Once upon a time": four simple and immensely powerful words. From a really early age we're exposed to the magic of storytelling. Since human beings first walked the earth, we've been sharing stories. Warning each other of mortal danger. Teaching right from wrong. Inspiring our tribe to action. The latest science tells us that when we hear a story our bodies produce the hormone oxytocin and we instantly start to form a connection with the person that we are listening to. Stories bind us together and help make sense of our experience.

We should know how to handle success and how to handle failures. Particularly if you are in a management position. Because any task you do, you will most likely come across problems. Problems should not become the captain of the individual or a project. The individual managing the project should be the captain of the problems and defeat the problems and succeed. Learning gives us creativity; creativity leads to thinking. Thinking provides knowledge; knowledge makes us great. History has proven that those who dare to imagine the impossible are the ones who break all human limitations. In every field of human endeavour, whether it be in science, medicine, sports, art or technology. The names of the people who imagined the impossible are engraved in our history. By breaking the limits of their imagination, they changed the world. For example, take Newton or Einstein. By breaking the limits of their imaginations, they changed the world. If you want to be discoverers, you want to be innovators. Inventions and discoveries have always been generated from creative minds. They have been constantly working and imagining the outcome in the mind. With the imagination and the constant effort all the forces of the universe work for that inspired mind. Thereby leading to inventions and discoveries.

It doesn't matter where the starting point is for you, it just matters where you finish and that's totally up to you. You have full control of your destiny. What I've learnt being around Mr Cox is how important it is to be conscious of the things you think about, the things you say and what goes in and out of your mind. The way he uses universal laws, I had to ask him, "Do you know anything about the universal principles and how they work?" "No," he replied. Further in the book I will lay out in detail what principle was used and how it was applied to help achieve his desired goals.

Not everyone wants to be a billionaire. The average person's definition of success is being financially free, owning a few properties across the world, having good debt instead of bad debt, going on holidays when they choose, not being confined to a 9-5 job where they have to go to work instead having the choice to spend time with their kids on their watch, and just not being worried all the time. You don't have to be a billionaire to have all these things, heck you don't even have to be a millionaire to be financially free. There's no secret to having all these things, it just takes planning and actions and following simple universal principles which anyone can use. The universe doesn't see race, age, sex, disability, it just recognises vibrations which we'll delve into further on.

Growing up in a poverty struck area, we never had role models to look up to. The role models we had were the people who engaged in unlawful acts and were in fact the root cause as to why the area was in the state that it was. Yet, seeing people who came from real poverty then go ahead to make a life for themselves, a decent life by the way, and share their story can give others hope. No matter where you are in life, the power of the mind can achieve anything that you can imagine.

Everyone looks for a way out of their current situation. When I mean everyone, I mean the population that struggles on a consistent basis and sees no end to financial difficulty. I know this book will give those individuals hope and inspire them to put in a little more effort than expected, to learn from every situation and to carry on when they feel like giving up.

Life wants you to be successful, but it's up to you if you want it. Life wants you to be happy, but it's up to you to pursue it. Life wants people to treat you well, but do you treat others well? Life wants you to live in abundance, but does your vibration match, or do you get in life what your thoughts attract? This book gives you a step-by-step guide of the universal principles and recounts the story of a man who unknowingly followed these principles to achieve his goal.

Once people realise that their reality is happening because of them and not to them, they can achieve self-awareness. When the reader then gains knowledge of oneself, this will then set off a chain reaction to their friends and loved ones.

Anything the human mind can believe; the human mind can achieve.

What is it that people want the most, wealth, fame, power, peace of mind, happiness?

The universal principles, if implemented correctly, can help you obtain anything you want in life. Although it's not easy, it's worth it. If gaining success was easy everybody on your street will be driving a Bentley. It's hard, that's a given.

This is a true story of a person who used the universal principles to get himself out of poverty. I'll note which principle was used, how he implemented it and how you can use it in your everyday life to change it for the better. The author will also compare and give examples of our 21$^{st}$ century role models. I was questioned if it is so simple to acquire anything you want in life by following principles that are out for everybody to learn for themselves. Why aren't there more successful people and why is poverty increasing in areas where there is unlimited wealth up for grabs? I will give you an example; why is Cristiano Ronaldo considered the greatest striker of all times? Even at his current age (34) he still manages to surpass expectations. Is it because he turns up for training before everyone else, maybe because he is the last to leave the training ground? Perhaps it is due to his consistent workout routine and diet plan, staying disciplined to his schedule. Maybe it's his vivid visualisation of what he wants to achieve in his football career. These are traits of the universal principles of success. Why aren't there more successful people with the amount of wealth that everyone has access to? The answer is simply because not everyone is willing to put in the work to obtain riches. Instead, the average person, puts in an average performance towards their work, personal and social life and expects results a millionaire would normally receive. This is not only just for sports, yes some are born with natural talents but the greatest work on their talent day in day out. You don't have to be the greatest if that's not something you desire. But if you give more effort than what is expected from you, you will soon reap the benefits. We live in a democracy where people just want to do enough just to get by and then go on to blame their surroundings, but rarely tackling the issue from the source which is ourselves.

Does being rich make you happier? That's the billion dollar question. Most experts on the matter agree that having certain freedom and securities that come with having lots of money does improve our sense of well-being. Psychologist

Daniel Kahneman and economist Angus Deaton concluded once you have an income over 58,000 GBP a year you won't necessarily become happier because of the cash, but it's the safety net and opportunities afforded to people that maintain a certain level of happiness. A life of penury is often full of fears and setbacks and having to see all the things in life you can't have. While rich folks are happier than poor folks, rich countries are not necessarily happier than poor countries.

How hard is it to get into the rich bracket? Well, it's hard. There's an old saying that the rich get richer, and the poor get poorer. Given that money begets money, unfortunately breaking out of poverty is no easy task. Wealthy households usually hang onto their wealth whereas less wealthy households tend to face all types of dilemmas. The average American family has $8,377 in debt and that means you'll be paying an interest on that; rich folks buy their goods outright for the most part and so as a poor person you continue being faced with borrowing fees. When you're struggling to pay for things outright, you are a prey not only to lenders but to the system also.

Are we meant to be who we are born? And that the rich stay rich and most of you will not be a part of that club? I would disagree!

# CHAPTER 1

## *Want*

> *"Desire is the starting point of all achievement, not a hope, not a wish, but a keen pulsating desire which transcends everything."* – Napoleon Hill

Mr Cox was born and grew up in St Elizabeth, Jamaica in the late 1960s. Mr Cox was the second of six children in the family. Growing up on a farm, the family never had that much disposable income. Not even for Mr Cox to have a pair of shoes to go to school in. Yes, travelling more than five miles just to go to school every morning and coming home in the evening barefoot, walking through stones, dirt and rubble. A few years later the family welcomed more kids, so money was tighter than ever before. Mr Cox's education was sacrificed, and he was sent to work on the farm before his teenage years. That was the last time he ever attended any form of education.

With no education, working countless hours on a farm, with scalding sun rays beating down on his body. No role model in sight, no future. You would have thought to yourself this is it; this is life for me. I need to accept my fate. If my father was doing this since he was a kid and his father before him was. How am I any different, I'm no better than them, am I?

How does someone who hasn't travelled any further than the school he went to as an infant know what else is out there? Put yourself in this position. You're brought up in the green and placid countryside. The people around you have no idea about agricultural development, where does one get the idea of wanting something better? Want! He wanted something better. He never knew how or why, he just wanted. So that was the first step. That is why I agree with Napoleon Hill when he said, "Desire is the starting point of all achievement, the first step towards riches." I find it truly remarkable how a kid from a third world country, struck with poverty started off his journey with him just wanting something better.

Something so simple and yet so effective. Why don't more people use the power of the mind to give them that drive to want a different life? Finding lesser wealthy people is easier than finding wealthy people. I took the pleasure of speaking to twenty different individuals who live hand to mouth, or live pay cheque to pay cheque. I'm not criticizing how they live. I myself used to fit in this category. So, I know how it is to be on both sides. I've written down six reasons why people didn't want to change. You can do the same thing and ask your friends or relatives who you believe may be in the same situation. See what you find are the most common reasons.

1. People just don't want to change

Maybe you think you want to change. But is it really your wish to? Or is this the wish of your parents, boss, partner, friends or society? If you don't want to make the change deep down, then it will be very difficult to go the distance. Yes, you can go the distance if there's no inner drive, but you will lose motivation easily and feel like giving up after a while.

Sit down and really think (meditate) about whose goals you are working towards. If they're not yours, stop working on them. Consciously spend time on your chosen goals instead. Brainstorm and write all your goals down, review that piece of paper and know why you want to achieve them and work towards them for your own sake.

2.   You don't feel bold enough
Change can be scary. Doing things for the first time or stepping into the unknown can be frightening. You may feel like you need some courage to make those changes you want, to take those first steps. You gain strength, courage and confidence by every experience in which you really stop to look fear in the face. You're able to say to yourself, "I have lived through this horror. I can definitely take the next thing that comes along." You must be willing to act, to move out of your comfort zone and to face fear to increase your courage and self-confidence in a way that stays with you. You know what they say about fear, it's just false-evidence-appearing-real.

3.   Your environment is holding you back
A few individuals I asked blamed their surroundings and said they're only a product of their environment. It's like saying, for example, if you're trying to lose weight then it will be a lot harder if the people around you are eating junk food. If you are trying to think more positively, it'll be a lot harder if you hang out with negative people all the time and watch the news and fear inducing tv-shows too much. Change your environment in a way that will support you. That doesn't mean you have to take drastic measures like never talking to some friends and family again to cultivate a more positive attitude. It may just mean cutting down on seeing negative people or tv-shows and replacing that by interacting with more positive people and positive media consumption. If you're trying to lose weight, then find people with similar goals that you can spend time with each week. Even if it's via online.

The same can be done with acquiring wealth.

4   Felt like giving up after a few failures
When you're young you don't really consider failure a huge thing. You learn to walk; you fall and knock your head and you get up again. The same goes for riding a bike. But through influence from school and society, failure becomes this increasingly frightening thing. Sure, as you get older the stakes get higher and you can lose a lot more if you fail. But you forget, most of the time the sky isn't going to fall if you fail. People will not mock you; life will just go on. But you must fail to gain this understanding. You will not get it by just reading these words and all other things by people who have said the same thing for centuries.
Your mind must experience failure or the possibility of it, over and over, to make the fear of failure a lot smaller. You may however find motivation in what failure teaches you. By adjusting your perspective, you start seeing failure as more of a learning experience.
*"Fears are nothing more than a state of mind."* – Napoleon Hill

5.   You don't feel enough pain yet
Oftentimes people just haven't had enough yet. When the pain of staying as you are become unbearable, you start looking for a positive way forward. Stop waiting for the problem to become too big. You can try to see your future vividly in your mind. Ask yourself where you want to be in five to ten years and where you are currently going. Then check yourself, are you making the right positive choices? Vividly seeing the inevitable consequences of not changing can be that nudge you need to get serious about improving something in your life.

6. You just don't know how to practically change.
This was the most common obstacle. Fortunately, we have the internet so it's a lot easier to find practical solutions to the problems many people have faced before you. Ask yourself, what have other people you know done in the past to improve their situation? Or if you can't find anyone, read books, articles, or blogs on the topic you need help on. But make sure you take advice from someone who has been in your shoes and has gone where you want to go. Find a way that suits you.

Working on a family farm, with no education and no money, how was Mr Cox going to obtain what he desired if nothing surrounded him but farmland and dead dreams? A thought? I've studied about the law of attraction and this comes to mind being in Mr Cox position. Where was he going to get an opportunity? But that did bother him. He knew in his mind what he wanted and that was good enough. Without education Mr Cox used the law of attraction. You can't control your surroundings, you can't help that the people around you have such small minds, you have no control of how your parents treated you whilst you were growing up. There is one thing you have full control over and no one can take away from you. Your mind.

Have you heard the saying "As a man thinketh, so he becomes"? So, in a man's own thought he creates the condition, good or bad, that enters his life. You've heard many of today's celebrities talk about the law of attraction. Denzel Washington said in an interview, "You attract what you fear." What he meant by that is you attract what's on your mind. I don't know how many people can disagree with that, ask any physicist and they'll tell you. Jim Carrey confessed to Oprah Winfrey, when he was broken and poor, he would visualise things he wanted in life and used his energy and emotion to feel it deeply. You must have an insurmountable belief in what you want and can achieve. He said, we are creators and we get what we desire when we really believe it. When we tune our energy to the right vibration, it comes to us in the most loving way possible. Now, everything that is going on in your current life, don't you feel you've somehow created it? From your thoughts or intentions perhaps? Nothing was accomplished without intention. Steve Harvey on the Steve Harvey show said that the book *The Secret* changed his life. Following the book's preaching, Steve Harvey affirmed that like attracts like. Therefore if you're negative you're going to attract negative and if you're positive you're going to attract positive. Thus, our thoughts are magnets and we attract the same things we feel inside. People will go on to say that this is common sense, but in our day and age, common sense isn't that common.

Despite every person saying the same thing when it comes to the law of attraction, there's one thing that they missed out on which I believe is the most important. If you don't do this then whatever you think about the most won't come into fruition without action. What's the use of thinking positive all day and just sitting there or laying in your sofa or bed and just concentrating on the hope of something good happening in your life? No! Sorry, it does not work like that. You think Mr Cox just worked on the farm from sunrise to sunset just expecting his thoughts alone to manifest his dreams? No. Life is simple but it's not that easy. Your mind can bring the opportunities towards your direction, but you need to act.

Mr Cox never thought about anything else, all he wanted was to elevate himself, he hated being on the farm seven days a week three hundred and sixty-five days a year. Regardless of not wanting to be in that position, he still cultivated those crops to the best of his ability. Mr Cox always did more than what was asked of him. Unknown to Mr Cox, there had been an agriculturalist in the area on business and he took a shine to Mr Cox's hard work. He approached Mr Cox and offered him a position on a farm in Iowa, in the United States of America. At this time Mr Cox's vocabulary was limited. He knew right there and then he was going to take the offer. Even though he was about to dive into the unknown by saying yes. This could have meant the beginning or the end of himself as he knew it. That's the difference between a person who really wants something and someone who is not too sure. Put yourself in Mr Cox's position. A man you never met approaches you and offers you a job in another country and tells you the boat leaves next week. Honestly, you'll say no, right? I would agree, I'll say no too. Consciously or unconsciously, he knew his thoughts created this opportunity. His thinking of wanting to move further than his current surroundings. The universe presented him with this opportunity, and he would be committing suicide to his dreams if hadn't said anything but yes.

Do you see how the law of attraction works, even though you have strong emotions and thoughts that you hold deeply? In order to bring it into reality, you must be willing to act upon what comes your way.

Here's some of the ways you can start to use the law of attraction.

Focus on what you want in life, not what you are lacking. Don't think about your old past time relationships, jobs, broken down car, financial poverty and ill health. Instead, picture yourself in a prospering relationship, in a career that you love and enjoy, a brand new car of your choice, being financially free, and being healthy. This puts the focus on what you want to bring to life, rather than what you want to eliminate. Doing so sends a message to the universe, saying that you expect good things to happen to you. The idea is, what you are thinking about is what you want in your life.

So, if you still think about the negative situations in your life, you're still then focusing on what you don't want and allowing the universe to grant you more of the thoughts you entertain.

When you want to manifest what you desire, try using more positive words. It's important you avoid using phrases that depend on negative words such as "no" or "not" to state what you want, such as "I don't want to lose my job." Similarly, don't include words for what you want to avoid attracting the wrong vibration. For instance, "I don't want to lose" sends out the word "lose" while "I want to win" sends out the word "win".

Visualise your dreams coming true. Close your eyes and picture yourself living the life you want. Imagine starting your business, imagine how it would feel to be with your ideal partner, imagine how your life would be if you had what you want. Do this everyday to solidify your intentions and bring them one step closer to reality. I will do a whole chapter on meditation to manifestation.

Upon arriving in Iowa, Mr Cox thought he had the world at his feet. A young countryside teenager who walked miles to school with nothing on his feet travelled on a boat from Jamaica to the United States of America: the land of opportunity. Mr Cox had no expectations of what was to expect, but he soon realised it wasn't all what it seemed to be. When he arrived on the farm, he soon came to the realisation that the American farmer wanted nothing more than a hard-working slave. The working days were long and strenuous, but with the currency exchange rate back then, the pay was higher. Mr Cox took the good with the bad.

I know a lot of the time most people would be discouraged about the situation. Leaving a nice hot country with fresh food, for the promise of a better life. You take a leap of faith, you go into the unknown only to find yourself working fifteen times harder than before. But not Mr Cox. When asked, "Did you have any regrets?" Mr Cox said, "No, of course not." Every situation whether good or bad we remember, and we learn from. I will go through more details about other situations later. Mr Cox was now surrounded by many more individuals, and had the opportunity to network. Even though a large proportion were in the same position as him, each one of them had different knowledge and Mr Cox knew by asking the right question he could now put the money he was about to save to beneficial use. Mr Cox didn't always enjoy his time picking tens of thousands of apples daily, being yelled out by a foreign person; this is what prison must have felt like. Although the unknown was not as welcoming as he thought, he knew there was something that no one was able to take away: his mind. No matter how unpleasant the position he was in. Mr Cox recognised it was temporary. He knew that he still wanted better and this was not the end. He knew what he wanted wasn't going to be easy to attain.

Have you ever felt like that every step you take, you're moving one step backwards instead forward to your goal? Just remember the powerful force of wanting, it drives our thoughts and emotions. This essence brings out strong emotions that send a high vibrational energy relating to what we are thinking. It was this driving force to find the missing link that kept Mr Cox going. There was no giving up. If his thoughts and actions brought him to the States. Maybe his growing desire of wanting more would elevate him to further heights. Not everyone would think like this and that is why not everyone has what they want in life. Mr Cox understood that nothing in life was going to be easy because he knew, easy come easy go.

*"You will fail your way to greatness."* – Les Brown

Most people give up on their dreams because of the rejections they get, but remember that at times rejection is necessary. It's no big deal. Rejection is just a myth. Think of it like this; every time you get turned away or you get that no, you are getting one step closer to that yes. You will only win if you don't quit, "even a broken clock is right twice a day."

Six months had passed and Mr Cox found himself back where it all started, back at the roads where he walked to school in his bare feet. Nothing much had changed in the area, or where Mr Cox was residing. Not in the physical world that is. Something had changed inside Mr Cox. Even though Mr Cox didn't get what he bargained for, Mr Cox had a look in his eyes his mother had never seen before. The first thing Mr Cox did when travelling back home, was not to waste his hard earned money on the bars, parties and buying clothes like all the other men who were on all the voyage back with him. He heard countless spiel of what others were going to do with the money they had earned from working 14 hours a day in Iowa. Someone saw that Mr Cox was quiet and asked him, "What are you going to do with your new wealth?" "Buy seeds." Mr Cox nodded. "Seeds?!" the man exclaimed and walked off.

Mr Cox had a religious mum, she could recite the Bible word for word, she always said that her son will be a saint one day. It was morning when Mr Cox arrived back to Jamaica, he hitched a ride to St Elizabeth and walked home from the nearest junction. Mrs Cox recognised her son walking over the horizon. She had hot soursop tea waiting for her son. Once settled he spoke with his mother, he told her the working conditions he went through and what he had to do for a routine. She praised the earths and the heavens that he had made it back in one piece. He then presented her with thousands of seeds he purchased at the market before arriving back to St Elizabeth. "Before I go back, I'm going to plant these; by the time I come back you can bear the fruit and can sell it to the supermarkets in the city." "Go back?" Mrs Cox uttered in confusion. "What do you mean go back?" "Go back to Iowa". It was at that moment Mrs Cox, knew her son had an intention of wanting, and her son would walk through thorn, stinging nettle bushes, step on crushed glass just to get to his port of call.

Give, and it will be given to you. A good measure, pressed down, shaken together and running over, will be poured into your lap. For with the measure you use, it will be measured to you Luke 6:38. The LORD will open the heavens, the storehouse of his bounty, to send rain on your land in season and to bless all the work of your hands. You will lend to many nations but will borrow from none. Deuteronomy 28:12.

I read the book called *The Secret* a few years back, a brilliant book. Rhonda Byrne really took me by surprise with the book and it has so far touched over a half of a billion people. Wow, I will be happy if my book reaches a twentieth of that. *The Secret* discusses the Law of Attraction and how to use it in your life. The book introduced many people to the concept that their thoughts may influence their actions, as well as the experiences that they bring into their lives. Although the book is empowering and encourages visualisation and boosts motivation, a lot of people do get confused. I've seen people complain because they think positive all day, they visualise what they want from the moment they awaken to the moment they drift off asleep, but why aren't their lives changing much, they wonder? Till this day the richest one percent of people still own more than half of this world's wealth. According to the credit Suisse global wealth report, the world's richest one percent, those with more than one million dollars own forty four percent of the world's wealth. The data also shows that adults with less than ten thousand dollars in wealth make up fifty six percent of the world's population but hold less than two percent of global wealth. Of the half of a billion people who read *The Secret* haven't wrapped their heads around how to really use it, otherwise these numbers would be a lot different.

I always found *The Secret* useful. Once perspective has changed, more choices over how we emerge and then inevitably, the way we feel about circumstances also changes. You can learn all techniques on how to be better. What's the point if you don't and go into action? How many people give up, how many let life beat them down, and are now stuck there? But you were thinking positive, weren't you? Why has life not bore fruit from the seeds you planted?

Every person who wins in any undertaking must be willing to burn his ships and cut all sources of retreat. Only by doing so can one be sure of maintaining that state of mind known as a "burning desire to win", essential to success.

As far as science has been able to determine, the entire universe consists of but two elements – matter and energy.

Through the combination of energy and matter, everything perceptible to man has been created, from the largest star which floats in the heavens, down to, and including man, himself.

You can build a fortune through the aid of laws which are immutable. But, first you must become familiar with these laws, and learn to apply them. Through repetition, and by approaching the description of these principles from every conceivable angle. I hope to reveal to you the secret through which every great fortune has been accumulated. Strange and paradoxical as it may seem, the "secret" is not a secret. Nature, herself, advertises it in the earth on which we live, the stars, the planets suspended within our view, in the elements above and around us, in every blade of grass, and every form of life within our vision.

# CHAPTER 2

## *State of Mind*

*Where attention goes. Energy flows.*

Poverty is just a state of mind. What you think about most is who you are and what you achieve. Move beyond limits to a mindset that attracts abundance. Often some will object to this, but your mind describes your mental wellbeing. Imagine having difficulties with your feelings and coping with everyday life can have a heavy burden on your mind, body and soul. After analysing hundreds of different individuals, a combination of age, religion, cultural background type of jobs and different incomes. The portion that had an unhealthy state of mind mostly felt sluggish, less confident and felt it was harder to nurture relationships. Your state of mind ultimately helps you with how you perceive life and how you react to certain situations. A healthy mind determines whether you are going to have an easier time coping with stress and means you're better at working more productively. You're capable of achieving much more with a healthy mind.

I often wondered about the fact that it takes so much more than just wanting something to achieve it. There are more principles to use if you want to achieve your goals. Wanting is only the beginning. Do you think by merely wanting something, you're going to get it with a snap of your fingers? No, my friend you're going to encounter countless obstacles. Studying Mr Cox, it was his state of mind that directed him through his trials and tribulations.

Few months had passed from having sailed back to Iowa, where less than fifty percent of the workers returned to the farm. The working conditions they went through were so unbearable that money wasn't a good enough excuse to return. This really hit home for me. It just goes to show that your goal has to be greater than all the hurdles you have to jump, and when you drop and fall it's your goal that's going to make you want to get back up again. I've seen countless men and women chasing their dreams, but as soon as they receive a couple of rejections, they admit defeat and lower their standards. If you want to become a actor or an actress, do you know how many auditions you have to go to? How many roles you have to play, which you wouldn't dare play even in your worst nightmares? Do you know how hard you must study if you want to be a doctor or a lawyer, days on end perfecting your craft? Pain is only temporary, but if you quit it will last forever.

Whatever your dream is, you must be willing to take the chance and most people won't even do that. Most people believe they have done all they are ever going to do, raise a family, earn a living and then they die. For people who are running toward their dreams, life has a special kind of meaning. Here's what I learnt and will share with you. In the process of working on your dreams, you are going to encounter a lot of disappointments, a lot of failure, a lot of pain, a lot of setbacks, a lot of defeats but in the process of doing that you will also discover some things about yourself that you don't know right now. What you will realise is that you have greatness within you. What you will realise is that you are more powerful than you can ever begin to imagine, what you will realise is that you are greater than your circumstances and that you don't have to go through life being a victim. Not only is it important that you believe and begin to know that it's possible for you to live your dream as you run towards it, but it's necessary that you work on yourself, that you develop yourself. It's necessary that you usher out the energy drainers out your life, so that you can live your dream.

Born in Lebanon to an English and American parents who quickly separated, Keanu Reeves spent most of his childhood moving around, with no stable family or place to live. His mother married three times and moved around the world. For the most part, he was raised by his grandparents and nannies. Dyslexic and disruptive, attending four different high schools, never ever graduating, one thing he did excel in was acting. Even when he finally got into Hollywood, he faced trials and tribulations; with his close friend Phoenix dying; losing a still born daughter, then losing his girlfriend in a car crash. Still, Keanu Reeves pushed through his acting career getting a star on the walk of fame and producing award winning films to this day. Don't get beaten by the situation because you will end up beating yourself, jeopardising your future in the process. When you dedicate your life to one goal, you don't care about the odds. When the dream is big enough the odds don't matter. If you don't control your environment, it's going to control you. Sudha Chandran was an aspiring dancer when she was sixteen. Soon after; she had an unfortunate accident while travelling in Tamil Nadu and was severely injured. She was taken to a local hospital for the initial treatment for her injuries, but her life took a sad turn when she was later admitted to Vijaya Hospital in Madras. Here, the doctors diagnosed the development of gangrene in her right leg and the conditions were so bad that the only way forward was to amputate her legs. The dancer grew accustomed to this tragedy and looked outside herself. Life gives no one special treatments because of their integrity. You must do what you have to do because that expresses who you are. Sudha Chandran still loves to dance and her clouds started to make way for the sunshine when she was given the prosthetic Jaipur foot. It had bestowed her with new life. In fact, she went on and became one of the most famous Bharatanatyam dancers of the Indian subcontinent. Sudha Chandran is fifty-five years old today and remains a success story, a star who has performed nationally and internationally. You see, if you dedicate yourself to a cause larger than yourself, you're not following the crowds. Most people are not intense about living. Nothing can resist the will of your state of mind.

When you believe and have a mind state of faith, you can perceive through anything. The secret to success is refusing to give up. Perseverance transforms average everyday working people into world champions. No matter what your goals are in life, there are going to be massive challenges, setbacks and heart breaking disappointments. Each of these circumstances might disguise themselves as failure. You must reject this lie and continue on to achieve your dream with even more determination. A lot has been spoken about this superwoman. Troublesome life as a child, but her story still astonishes and inspires us. Once victim of child sexual abuse by relatives and family friends, a mother at the age of fourteen whose child passed away in just two days, a vicious prey to racism, bullied for her body type, she continued to bust her butt through high school and earned a full scholarship to college. From a local network anchor in Nashville to becoming an owner of her own network. Oprah Winfrey is truly one of the best examples who worked diligently to achieve success, even if she had to walk through fire and brimstone to execute her success. Oprah has been deemed the most influential woman on the planet. She has been awarded the presidential medal of freedom by former president Barack Obama. She has been ranked the richest African American in the twentieth century and the greatest black philanthropist in American history.

This just goes to show that, no matter what type of beginning you possibly came from, success does not discriminate. Success is a state of mind. If you want success, start thinking of yourself as successful. Was Mr Cox furious that he had to stay an extra six month on the fields, the answer is no he wasn't. Since I was a child, I gathered that his state of mind was to always spot the positive in every situation.

The benefits of a positive attitude can:
1. Help you achieve goals and attain success;
2. Bring more joy into your life;
3. Make you a pleasant person to be with, and make it easier to be liked amongst network partnerships;
4. Cultivate more energy, enthusiasm, interest, and even curiosity, making life more interesting;
5. Increase your confidence in your abilities, and bring hope and expectation of a brighter future;
6. Enhance your motivation when carrying out tasks and working on goals, and you are also able to inspire and motivates others.

These weren't the ultimate key factors to Mr Cox, but without his positive attitude when he started out on his path to chase a dream of wealth, he would have been less persistent. The first step, the first day, the first minute; you're excited. The next day comes and you're like "Man, this is a little tough." And then you take another step and another step then maybe a few days down the line and then you're like "This is pretty hard, man." and then what happens is the enthusiasm from the beginning of the process starts to fade out. Motivation is a very fickle thing and successful people learn you can't rely on motivation alone. Successful people learn how to function with or without it every single day. Go out there and you do your best. If you do the same things you did yesterday, you're not improving, and you'll never change your life.

Everyday you have to begin to recondition your mind. Good things are supposed to happen to you. Say that to yourself everyday. We now live in a world where we believe that bad things are supposed to happen to us. Why do we have a mentality that this is too good to be true, that something bad is bound to happen? Then guess what, it does! Watch your words, watch what you say about yourself, be conscious of what you think daily. "Why?" Because your words are powerful. Life and death are in the tongue, watch what you say, never say "I'm broke." Say "I'm overcoming a cash flow problem". Claim what you want not what you don't want. So, say to yourself that good things are supposed to happen and begin to believe that, begin to expect that.

Let me ask you something, do you expect to be successful? Given the fact that you're a single parent. Given the fact you decided not to go to university to further your education. Given the fact that you're very talented, but falling behind on your dreams and your bills. Do you expect, based on your current performance, to be successful? If you ask most people, "Do you want to be successful? Do you want to live a life of productivity? Do you want to live a life of contribution? Do you want to be a better parent to your kids? Do you want to have your own business? Are those the dreams that you want?" Everybody will say, "Yes." But what shows up in conversation, is different to what shows up in behaviour. See, you can always tell what someone expects by what someone does. Judge a tree by the fruit it bears, not the fruit that it wants. Not the fruit that it claims. What do you do behind the scenes; when no one is watching? Your behaviour, how do you conduct yourself? Do you write your goals down? Decide to find some product, or an idea, some service that you can provide, that you can begin to create value for yourself. In order to generate wealth. It's very important we learn how to begin to create wealth. I'm not talking about loving money. I don't believe money is the route of all evil. I believe the lack of money is the route of all evil. People will steal for money; some people will even kill for money. People are willing to sit down in a prison cell for money. Every time unemployment goes along up, crime always goes up with it. Everybody wants to be comfortable in life, studying all the millionaires and successful people in the world. People say money won't make you happy, but everybody wants to find out for themselves.

Self-hypnosis is an ideal way to begin to change the state of your mind. First, what is self-hypnosis? Self-hypnosis or auto-hypnosis is a form, a process, or the result of a self-induced hypnotic state where the individual can achieve and accomplish their fullest potential. This craft has been taught to people all over the world so they can gain control of their lives, feel inspired, empowered and fulfilled. Athletes, business students and entrepreneurs are the top profession in which the use of self-hypnosis occurs the most.

Therefore, ask yourself if you could use this technique. What would you accomplish? If you are just starting on your journey towards your dreams, stop to think for a little while. How could you achieve your full potential? In this process, I want you to develop a better picture of yourself. Before the process, ask yourself what you want to gain from this. If you're a student, maybe you want to get better grades, eliminate exam anxiety or develop a superpower memory. If you're in business, perhaps this will help you be more productive and in result make more money, but I want you to understand that it all starts with how you think. Studies shows that many people go to bed stressed and wake up worried and anxious. Admit it, even you have gone to bed stressed and woke up anxious about something. Absolutely, every single person has. That's one of today's problems in society. When we are not thinking good about ourselves, we're not feeling good and when we are not feeling good, we're not doing good. Thereupon, what I want to teach the readers and this is what Mr Cox used so well on his journey to success, is how to control your thoughts and programme your mind as you would a very highly efficient powerful computer. Who wouldn't like that?

Before I go into detail about how to use this tool, recognise that you're already telling yourself that something has programmed you. You've been exposed to programming and hypnotised since you existed in the womb. You have been exposed to hypnosis not only by society, not just by religion, not only by advertisers, not only by your peers, parents but also by yourself. So, you're already telling yourself something and that is created by telling yourself a thought. That thought creates a feeling for yourself and then that feeling creates an action and that then also influences your body. Now as I was explaining earlier, we really do become what we think about. If you picture this, you're walking into college and you have a test to take that day, your teacher before told you that it was going to be the most difficult test you've ever taken. Then now you have that in your mind, you've created that thought, and you're thinking to yourself no matter how much you study, you're destined to fail. Unfortunately, a lot of people are sending those messages to other people outside of their realm. It's time to control it, to eliminate that external programming and learn how to start programming ourselves. To start thinking better so we can start feeling better, to start feeling better so we can start acting better. How are we not taught to learn how we become what we think about?

Follow along with me for a moment, if you can take your hands. Lock them together. Take your two index fingers and point them out. As you do this, I want you to count to three and I want you to do three things. On the count of three, I would like you to separate your two index fingers, look at them and then take these words in. One, two, three, separate your fingers. Look at them, they're going to touch. Imagine what it would be like if two rubber bands were attached to your fingers, pulling them closer and closer together. Imagine what it would be like for magnets to be attached to your fingers pulling them closer and closer together. Closer and closer together until they touch. The space between your fingers gets smaller and smaller. It may happen slowly, it may happen fast, but when your fingers touch and you take them apart, they'll touch faster the second time. Now, take your hands apart. I know it's a freaky feeling, but shake them out. If that worked for you, you've just been hypnotised. That's all it is. I find that people have this fear about hypnosis, that they think it's mind control or the work of the devil. They think that it's sleeping or being unconscious, but going into hypnosis every single day, several times a day. If you drive, think about this. You are driving to your destination, all of sudden you zoned out and you wound up at your destination and don't even remember how you got there. That's called road hypnosis, how about this. You see somebody texting on their mobile phone, you are walking, and that person is so focused on that text message you start talking to them, but they have no clue on what you are saying. This is hypnosis. Hypnosis is just an altered natural zoned focus state and the idea is to learn how to use this effectively. At night as we fall asleep, we go into a natural zoned state. A natural receptive state and just like the previous exercise. Were you thinking about something and it happened, you see your thought became one with your body thoughts and actions? For the last five minutes before you are falling asleep, when you fall asleep you go into a natural receptive state. So, you can use that receptive state. For the last five minutes you're falling at night, instead of worrying about what's going to happen tomorrow or being anxious about what's going to happen next week, I want you to think of what you want to accomplish that week, month or year. Make a little movie in your mind of what ideal scenario would like, if this idea sounds a little intimidating, just think about what you want tomorrow to be like. How you want tomorrow to go. If you have something that will otherwise stress you out, let's say maybe going for a job promotion or a job interview, maybe going in to take a test or an exam and you think naturally you normally will be stressed out about this. See yourself at night as you fall asleep, going into that job interview with your head held high and imagine what'll it be like for you landing that job. If you're taking a test, imagine walking into that testing room, filling out the exam with the best of your abilities, using that as an opportunity to show what you know and walking out knowing that you did well. When you begin to formulate this picture in your mind you have a better chance of things going that way. As you fall asleep at night, go into that focused zone state. So, let's use it, let's start thinking better of ourselves and when we start thinking better, we will start feeling better, when we start feeling better, we start doing better. When you do this technique at night, it will only around five minutes. Practice this, try it out, successful people make this their ritual. When you fall asleep at night, make a little movie in your head on how you want tomorrow to go or how you want to be as your ideal self. It could be a goal you have in mind. It could be something you just like to accomplish and do better at. When you play that picture over and over in your mind, it will more likely become your reality and thus, you have hypnotised yourselves. To the casual observer, it looks like you are just putting someone to sleep, but by doing this exercise you are actually waking up a part of your mind. As a result, you're also awakening within you hidden skills, attributes, resources and talents that you may not have known you had at your disposal and you can start using this to your benefit.

Countless celebrities and business tycoons have spoken about their success stories and how affirmations are a huge part of it. Just like these famous people, you too have the power to gain complete control over your dream. Denzel Washington, an A-list Hollywood star is indebted to affirmations for his skyrocketing success. He got over his drinking problem that was holding back his mind and his body from achieving greater things, with the help of his positive mindset he started believing in his own craft and made it to the top. Jennifer Lopez the mega popstar reveals that her day is incomplete without at least fifteen minutes dedicated to affirmations. She has always said that it's affirmations that have brought in success for her and helps her stay grounded.

It wasn't a surprise when Mr Cox first told me that he uses self-hypnosis still to this day. It was more of an eye-opener when he used this when he was much younger. Currently, a lot of people seek outside help to achieve this technique, but Mr Cox started using this skill when he was a teenager. I can now see how he remained strong in all the life tests he had to face. Positive affirmations and thoughts shaped Mr Cox's life in an amazing way, and his ability to stay positive and maintain a positive mind state determined the tone for his emotional life. The words you used to describe what is happening to yourself trigger the emotions for external events. Mr Cox always saw things positively and constructively; he saw the good in every situation he encountered. Naturally tending to remain cheerful and optimistic. Mr Cox knew that the quality of his overall life was determined by how he feels moment to moment. One of your most important goals should be to use positive affirmations to keep yourself thinking and talking about what you want and to steer your mind away from what you don't want or what you fear.

Mr Cox was a young boy, walking miles every morning and every evening to and from school in nothing but his bare feet, just to get the most basic education known to man. Having to do this for a few years only just to go and work on his father's farm to help put food on the family table. Others would have seen this as a burden, but the power of Mr Cox's state of mind always helped him keep a smile on his face. Knowing he never went to bed hungry, he exuded gratitude for the things he currently had. He knew it would give him the edge to achieve more in life. Mr Cox always knew he was going to be wealthy. People will say, "How did a poor child in a third-world country know he was going to be wealthy?" Mr Cox would have never classed himself as poor because his state of mind was always focused on abundance. Abundance is more than just prosperity or money, it's an energy of infinite happiness, success, love, health and all good things.

After Mr Cox's second trip to the States, he focused on his state of mind. He didn't let the situation hold him back. He knew he couldn't control his environment, but there was one thing he could control: what he thought of the situation. Anytime Mr Cox was faced with an unpleasant situation, he would focus on solving the issue and not concentrate on the negative side, which helped him cope with stress faster and more effectively. It's proven that people who think more positively live longer and feel better than people who don't. Mr Cox's journey to a wealthy life needed the best health possible which started from the mind. Instead of focusing on your failures, concentrate on life opportunities.

We can complain because rose bushes have thorns, or rejoice because thorns have roses.

# CHAPTER 3

## *Belief*

Keep your dreams alive. Understand that achieving anything requires faith and belief in yourself along with vision, hard work, determination and dedication. Remember all things are possible to those who believe.

Somewhere deep inside, you know the person you were designed to be. What kind of seed was planted in you? I believe part of our responsibility in life, is to find out who we are. To discover ourselves. First, we need to respect our nature. We need to realise we are part of a continuous chain that carries legacy and responsibility and if that is the case, we need to recognise that we are not biological coincidences. Second, we need to know our nature, to know ourselves. Know things about yourself that most people don't discover. For example, know how smart you are. Not how smart you are in comparison to others. In what ways are you smart, what do you care about? What are the values that motivate your choices? Know what your personal velocity is. Know what your drive is and how you naturally operate. Know your behaviour and how you come across to other people. Know the pattern in your choices so you learn more about what it's like to be you, so you can do an even better job.

Having faith does not solely transform you, but you transform the world as we know it today. You and I were born with a gift to make this world a better place. Even if we don't improve, we can encourage people, compliment people, solve problems, fix things, bring new ideas. But as you grow, you become a bigger source for the rest of life to grow to express itself through you. You were put here for a reason, so nurture your nature. Believe that you are valuable, accept that, know who you are and how you can understand you better; then apply yourself to the world. Work in such ways the world looks at you and says, "If he or she could do it, I could probably do it. I wonder how they did it. Then we start spreading that and then the ripple goes worldwide. Ask yourself every day, "How would the person I would like to become do the things I'm about to do?"

Sometimes we agonise over deciding, some decisions are major decisions and also a lot of small decisions we don't make. They tax our minds, they drain our energy, they create a lot of anxiety and nervousness because we don't take care of it. We decide not to decide which is a decision. Deciding to decide, to act, is a major challenge for all of us. It's a challenge in different ways and different areas of our lives. Some things happen to us along the way, experiences that prevent us from working through the mental block that stops us from acting. From doing the things we ought to do. So, what I want you to think about is what you know you need to do. Something that you want to do, but for some reason or another you've been holding back; for some reason or another you just haven't been able to gather your nerves to start, or have not been able to work through the procrastination. Something you haven't done, for which you just keep making excuses, even when you know you want to do it. But you don't know why you haven't done it. I know this is not easy. It is very challenging to act. From acting there is a fear of failure and if you've already failed, you don't want to fail again. The disappointment. The fear of loss is another thing. Many of us don't act because we want other people's approval. Many of us don't do the things we know we should do due to the lack of confidence; we don't believe in ourselves. There are many reasons why we don't act. There are also other things that infect us, not wanting to take personal responsibility, we want someone else to do it. Many times, we pick up our inability to do certain things from people that we love. People that we admire. We identify with them and we live in their context of their ideas, their opinions, and their life patterns. We buy into it unconsciously.

You must jump, you got to take the leap of faith. Some of you need to walk or jump off that cliff; out as far as you can. Now a lot of times you stand on the cliff of life and you see other people soaring by. Gliding down like a bird flying; you know they're going over to the south of France. You see them on boats somewhere, you see them on family vacation here and then vacationing there. You see them in New York then you see them in London, they're flying by, you know why? Because their parachute opened. The only way to get your parachute to open so you could soar, is you must jump! But here is the problem my friend. When you jump, I can assure you one thing, when you jump your parachute will not open right away. that's the scary part. You are going to hit them sides and injure your back out on them rocks, you're going to cut yourself, you're going to end up getting wounded but eventually your parachute will open. If you do not jump, I promise you one thing, your parachute will never open. On the other hand, you'll be safe, but you'll never soar. You must jump.

Faith consists of believing when it is beyond the power of reason to believe.

It was the nineteen nineties; Mr Cox had done his final trips to the States to work for his hard earned dollar. His father's farm was up and running, cultivating acres of fruit and vegetables. The family is more than capable enough to feed off the land for the foreseeable future. Mr Cox raised up one early morning, before anyone else in the house. Normally his parents are already up watering the outside plants or taking a morning stroll. Mr Cox slept head to toe with his younger brother, who was a few years younger than him. Being only a teenager still Mr Cox wanted his own place to call home, different from the home he was living in currently. Mr Cox got out of bed, put his slippers on and went straight out the back gate, trying not to wake anyone in the process. Where the family lived it was surrounded by acres of land. Above them was a hill with just over one point five-acre worth of untouched land that was impossible to cultivate. Mr S G Cox stared at the top of hill for fifty-seven minutes, he heard the roosters in the background signalling it was the rise of the sunshine and his mother would be up anytime soon. Mr Cox nodded his head to himself and said, "This is where I'm going to build my home. On top of this hill is where my home will lay."

Mr Cox didn't know how he was going to be able to build his dream house on the top of the hill. He didn't know when. He knew he was going to build his home, that all he knew. He had a bigger dream and he believed he would build his home in the up and coming years.

Sometimes the difference in whether you succeed or whether you don't comes down to one simple thing – believing in yourself. Have you ever thought about how much believing in yourself makes a difference in the quality of life? Think about it for a minute. If you don't really believe that you can do something, you are not going to give your full effort. And without your full effort, your chances of successfully achieving your goal are greatly reduced.

Whatever the mind can conceive you can achieve. These are just a finite number of reasons why believing in yourself is essential in your journey to success:
- You recognise your own ability to accomplish your goals;
- You're a lot more optimistic about the future;

- Deep down inside, you know you can do anything. Which makes you take the first step in walking toward your dreams;
- You treat yourself kindly, making your outlook on life much brighter;
- You feel uplifted and more satisfied with life;
- You're motivated to get things done;
- You naturally attract other like-minded people around, which can help boost morale and achieve your goal in a more abundant fashion.

Ideas are very powerful, it's not only emotions that are very powerful in human life. Psychoanalysis has examined the emotional basis of human opinions and beliefs, but we should also examine the intellectual basis psychological principles and theories.

The first thing which determines whether you can do something or not, is potential. For example, Roger Bannister was the first person to run a four-minute mile. He didn't physically practice. He made a shift in his mind. He practiced it in his head because he could never do it physically. When the result became certain enough, he believed it and then his body got him through. After Roger Bannister ran that four-minute mile, within two years thirty-seven people ran a four-minute mile, when no one in history had ever done it prior. Most people have a belief of what their potential is no matter what you or I tell them. That in turn affects what action they take and of course and that affects their result. Then, ironically, that result reinforces their belief. I want you to think about a major goal that you know you want, or maybe it's one you're already working on. You have experienced a lot of setbacks, a lot of defeats, you've experienced a lot of disappointment, maybe you have already given up and maybe you just need a little push, a little encouragement to get back up in the game again. Here's what I want you to look at. There are winners, there are losers, and there are people who haven't yet discovered how to win, and all these individuals need are some coaching. All they need is some help and guidance, just a little support. All they need is some insight or adjustments that will give them the key to open a whole new future for them. That will give them access to the unlimited power that they have within themselves. That's all they need. So, what I want you to do is think about something you want for you. That's real for you. That's important for you. That will give your life some special meaning. I don't want you to say, "I can do that"; I don't want you to assume that. Just say it's possible. Every time you look at your dream just say it's possible. Say that everyday to yourself; it's possible. What does that do? It begins to change your belief system. The way we operate is this: we manifest what we believe is possible for us. Whatever you have done up until this point; all that it really is, is a reproduction of what you subconsciously believe what you deserve and what's possible for you in life. You know in your heart that if someone has done it, then you can do it. It's possible, and if someone can make their dream a reality, it is also possible that you can make your dream a reality.

Mr Cox didn't know how he was going to build his dream, but the belief that it was possible was more than enough to give him the confidence to go ahead after what he sought. Every day he was thinking about his dream till it became an obsession. A friend had told Mr Cox about a place called London, Great Britain. He indicated with so much emotion how foreigners over the world came to this destination and amassed a fortune and then invested it back in their own homeland. Without even hesitating in Mr Cox's mind, he knew to himself that Great Britain is where he is going to end up. Mr Cox had cousins in that part of the world that coincidentally were coming to Jamaica for a summer holiday.

Mr Cox didn't want to sound desperate as he didn't want anyone to use him. So, he sent a message to them via another family member. The message was that he would be their personal guide, that he would take them on a full tour of Jamaica, the best tourist spots, the best bars and whatever their interest were he would find a spot to suit their needs. The message from Mr Cox was received and the recipients were more than happy to have one of their little cousins show them around the country from which their heritage was.

Beverley and Angela, Mr Cox's cousins, were truly grateful for the experience, they never imagined they would have had the opportunity to have so much exposure to their home country. They wanted to reward their cousin with financial gains. Mr Cox said thank you, but no thank you. Initially they were surprised due to Jamaicans having the habit of trading time for money. Mr Cox simply asked for sponsorship. They told Mr Cox that the UK wasn't a walk in the park, Mr Cox simply replied, "If you can thrive in the jungle, you can thrive anywhere." They said the UK was not a holiday destination. He nodded his head, "I know that." They felt indebted to him, but this was a big ask from Mr Cox. So, they offered him a counteroffer. The pair had a spare room in their property which needed tenanting. They agreed, they would get Mr Cox a visa to come to the UK. They also had a job for him when he landed but he had to give them twenty percent of his wages on a weekly basis. Without any doubt Mr Cox agreed.

The fundamental key to success is what you believe is true for yourself. You want it, then you must believe. You can say to yourself you want to be the most successful person in the world. But if you believe there is a glass ceiling in your way, you will be defined by the glass ceiling that is in your way.

Three months have passed in living in the UK, the way

things were going Mr Cox couldn't keep up with what he's doing if he ever wanted to build his dream life. Grateful for the opportunity to be out in a place where anyone can become a success with the right mindset and work ethic, but he was being held back. More than twenty percent of his wages were being taken. He soon realised he wasn't best pleased being taken advantage of. For now, he would do what needed to be done, but at any spare time he got for himself, he spoke to strangers, learned from them, picked their brains, networked. Mr Cox became friends with a lady who was a nurse in training who took a fancy to his accent. They hit it off. This became one of his first true friends since leaving home. He explained to her why and how he came to England. She commended him and respected his work ethic. She was having trouble keeping up with her rent, therefore she was looking for a house mate. Mr Cox's living position wasn't too great, he didn't even have his own room. He was living in a cupboard underneath the staircase. He never slept straight as the room wasn't long enough for his whole body. Anything is better than where he is living now.

Three months went by and everyone who came across Mr Cox took a liking to him. He was helpful, friendly, hard-working. Honest people just naturally gravitated towards him. He was offered a taxi role, but Mr Cox had no idea what this would entail of him. Mr Cox walked with the cab service owner, he laid out what Mr Cox needed to become a taxi driver. Mr Cox asked why. The answer was simple. "You are a hard worker. You work with a purpose, but where you currently are, I know you're not earning what you could if you join the taxi business. You get a set salary; work here and you will earn what you put in. Have a think and get back to me". Mr Cox didn't need anytime to think about the decision he was going to make. It was a move up, even though Mr Cox knew in order to earn he had to invest in himself. The money he originally had saved up for was getting the infrastructure started on his home back in Jamaica. Mr Cox knew, in order to earn more he had to learn more. Two months later he did just that. With the very little Mr Cox had to himself, he would study the A-Z, familiarizing himself with every road in London. Mr Cox never had an education, but he was extremely talented in agriculture and map reading. Mr Cox passed his driving test before he knew it. Mr Cox went back to the taxi stand to speak with the owner, he showed that he passed the test and said he was ready to start. The cab owner could see how eager Mr Cox was. He personally assisted him with obtaining his public carriage office licence and purchasing a suitable vehicle in order to officially start.

Success is not obtained overnight. It comes in instalments; you get a little bit today, a little bit tomorrow until the whole package is given out to you. The day you procrastinate, you lose that day's success. I know bettering ourselves can be very difficult, but I think it is still possible. If we don't like something about how we are, we have the power to change it.

Tyler Perry was one of four children, he had a very difficult and rough childhood, for years, he suffered brutal physical abuse from his father and severe sexual abuse from several adults. He once described his father as a man "whose answer to everything was to beat it out of you." One time, whilst his mother was out, he described the beating from his father. He got the vacuum cleaner extension cord and trapped him in a room and beat him until the skin was coming off his back. "To this day, I don't know why a person would do something like that to a child. "But thank God, in my mind, I left. I didn't feel it anymore. I learned to use my gift, as it was my imagination that let me escape." Tyler Perry was five or six years old the first time he was molested.

He later endured sexual molestation from a male nurse and a man he knew from church. When he was ten years old, he was also molested by a friend of his mother. Growing up, Tyler says he never felt safe. After one of the many vicious beatings from his father, Tyler blacked out for three days. Every single day, he lived in agonizing fear that something would make his father angry. His living conditions and his depression got so bad, that young Tyler took drastic measures. At one point, he even attempted suicide by slitting his wrists. This was an effort to escape his difficult situation. In his twenties, he eventually forgave his father, though his father never apologized. When he was sixteen, he changed his first name to Tyler to divide himself from his father. He also dropped out of high school, but later he earned a general equivalency diploma before discovering what his true passion was. He held a series of unfulfilling jobs. One time, Perry was very inspired by one comment while watching an episode of Oprah Winfrey's talk show, how writing about difficult and rough experiences could lead to personal development. Because of that, he started writing a series of letters to himself, which became the foundation for the musical *I know I've been changed*. Later in nineteen ninety-two he wrote, produced and starred in his first theatre production, *I know I've been changed*. In that moment, into that show Tyler Perry put all his savings. But it failed miserably. The run lasted just one weekend and only thirty people came to watch the show. But he didn't give up. He kept up with the production. Because of that, he had to work more odd and unfulfilling jobs and had to sleep in his car just to get by. But six years later. On its seventh run, the show finally became a success and opened huge doors for him. Since then, Perry continued his extremely successful and fulfilling career as a director, writer, and actor. In fact, in two thousand and eleven, Perry was named Forbes' highest paid man in entertainment. Tyler Perry made seventeen movies in ten years, which have a lifetime gross of about eight hundred and forty-five million dollars worldwide, with seven television shows, twenty stage plays and a New York times best-selling book. "One of the most difficult things about being a dreamer is the fear that the dream will never happen. I'm here as a living witness to tell you your dreams can come true. You can't give up. And I am here to let you know that everything can work together for your good. The time that you are spending on that job, that you think is a dead end, but it is not. You're being prepared just like I was. I was a shoeshine boy, I worked as a bill collector, a used car salesman, in housekeeping in a hotel, and they all were preparing for where I am now. What do these things have to do with where I am now? I'm glad you asked. I can use skills that I learned. I shined shoes, so I know how to shine my shoes If I need them to look nice. Selling used cars was a great way to learn how to close a deal. Bill collecting taught me great negotiation skills. Working at a five-star hotel taught me a lot about travel. Every experience in your life is here to teach you something. Today while you're at work, don't get frustrated. Look around you and ask God what you are there to learn and how it will be a part of your future dream. Honour that job, do the best you can at it, because God will bless you for honouring something that belongs to another. You have to understand what you may perceive to be a failure may very well be an opportunity to learn, grow, get better, and prepare for the next level. If you find the lessons in what you perceive to be failures, then you won't ever fail at anything."

The question you have to ask yourself isn't "Can I handle the situation?" The question is "Can I handle my mind?" Can you manage the thoughts and emotions that are trying to poison your progress? Forget managing the situation.

Manage your mind. Doesn't matter who is at fault, it is that something is broken. It's your responsibility to fix it. It's not somebody's fault if somebody's father was an abusive alcoholic, but it's for damn sure their responsibility to figure out how they are going to deal with those traumas and try to make a life out of it and try. It's not your fault if your partner cheated and ruined your marriage, but it's for damn sure your responsibility to take that pain and think about how to overcome that and build a happy life for yourself. Fault and responsibility do not go together. When something is somebody's fault we want them to suffer, we want them punished, we want them to pay. You want it to be their responsibility to fix it. That is not how it works, especially when it's about your heart, your life, your happiness. In that case, it's your responsibility and your responsibility alone.

Men with negative minds tried to convince Thomas A. Edison that he could not build a machine that would record and reproduce the human voice, "Because," they said, "no one else has ever produced such a machine." Edison did not believe them. He knew that they could produce anything the mind could conceive and believe, and that knowledge was the thing that lifted the great Edison above the common herd.

Men with negative minds told George Washington he could not hope to win against the vastly superior forces of the British, but he exercised his divine right to believe, therefore a great nation was born under the stars and stripes and the doubters have all been forgotten.

If you genuinely want more out of life, chances are you're not really going to fit in anywhere because the majority of people settle for average. And if you don't drop down to their level there's going to be conflict, they won't like the fact that you're going to commit to your dream. Because it reminds them that they gave up on theirs. One of the biggest reasons most people don't follow through with their dream life, is that they fear they would be left out of their circle if they achieved it. This is conscious or unconscious, but most people give up. Not because they can't make it. Not because they aren't capable, but because they are surrounded by people who have settled. People who don't want to see you succeed, because that would remind them that they didn't. They might start saying, "You've changed since you became successful." Not understanding that your goal was always to change. To develop, to reinvent yourself. You will hear ridiculous comments like "Successful people are greedy." My favourite one is: "There's more to life than money."Of course, there's more to life than money, but there's also more to life than struggling to pay bills and put food on the table. So much negativity towards the successful and the sad part is they would never be successful with this mentality. You ask ninety nine percent of successful people how they achieved their dream life; I can assure you the story will be the same. They worked harder than the majority, they kept going when the majority gave up, they suffered through failure but made sure that that was not the end. Rather a lesson learned. They went through hell but always focused on the end goal. Sadly, most people would rather argue about their limitations than accept there are no limitations. Most people would rather hate the successful ones than learn from them. Most people would rather pick up a beer, rather than a book. Then they'll complain that they're in a dead-end job or complain that they got laid off from their job. If they made the right decisions early on, they wouldn't have to clean up their bad decisions later. Most people would rather party now and suffer later. Maybe that's why most people are not where they want to be. Maybe that's why most people complain, maybe that's why most people live with regret. If you are most people commit right now to becoming a minority. Set your goals, right now. Don't you waste another moment of your life. Find a mentor, or a book, or a person, and learn from them, model them. Read, develop your mind. Reinvent yourself, make a commitment to be different, make a commitment to never give up on your goals, your dream life, your vision. Your future self is begging you to make that commitment, your future self is begging you to stick it out.

Belief is what made Mr Cox act into chasing his dream, belief is what made Mr Cox walk through hell because he believed from a young age every man and woman abled or disabled was meant to have an abundant life. He knew we were not put here to be stuck in the situation we find ourselves in but to learn from them, to better ourselves. Mr Cox was faced with a small dilemma. His visa was only permitted for twelve months. Mr Cox was now ten months into the duration of his stay. There was no way he could leave now. He just had the foundation done for his house in Jamaica. The taxi business was booming, and he started to grow fondly of Jane. They both understood each other. Their burning desire to achieve their goals.

It was just like any other day; Mr Cox had just dropped a passenger off to Paddington Station. Just after Mr Cox inserted his keys in the ignition, he saw another car heading straight in his direction. Given the amount of time Mr Cox had to react, he only could put up his hand brake and brace himself for a full-on collision. The unknown man had collided with Mr Cox vehicle head on. Airbags in both cars exploding straight away. The impact of the crash and Mr Cox head thrusting on the back of the head rest going into the other direction face first in the airbags knocking him unconscious. When Mr Cox had finally woken up, he was clueless to where he was, he never saw groups of white folks in white dressing gowns rushing everywhere before. Unknown to his current predicament and forgetting about the crash that had taken place, momentarily Mr Cox panicked; he was going into shock. A nurse injected him with general anaesthetic, relaxing and calming. Several hours later, after Mr Cox's forehead was stitched and his bruises and sprains were treated, the medication was wearing off. Mr Cox's memory slowly started coming back to him. A nurse explained to him what had happened. A uniformed man with a badge across his vest approached Mr Cox's hospital bed. "How are you doing, sir? Can you just confirm your name for me?" "Spurgeon Cox." "Thanks. We've done a name check and your visa has run out." Mr Cox couldn't believe what he was hearing, while the officer was talking in the background. All he could do was think to himself, "Why, why, why? I was going to get that dealt with. Why did that man have to crash into me?" The officer was still explaining what was going to happen after he was released from the hospital. Mr Cox was unaware of what he was hearing, he was becoming lightheaded, his heart monitor started to drop, pulses started to drop, lower by the second, alarm rings started going off. Alerting the nurses and doctors, Mr Cox had blacked out.

Mr Cox had woken up for the third time since the nightmare of a crash that took place. Hoping this was all a dream. Tears started rolling down from his eyes, trying to wipe his tear drops off with his right hand, he realises his right hand was handcuffed to the hospital bed. This wasn't a nightmare. It was his reality. He was to be deported back to Jamaica.

You got a dream? You got a vision? I won't lie to you, it is going to cost you everything. You're going to hurt in place that you didn't know could hurt. You'll have a thousand chances to give up. But don't do it. Keep on moving. Pick your associates more carefully because it does have an impact with your success.

*"If you think you are beaten, you are,*
*If you think you dare not, you don't*

*If you like to win, but you think you can't,
It is almost certain you won't.
"If you think you'll lose, you're lost
For out of the world we find,
Success begins with a fellow's will-
It's all in the state of mind.
"If you think you are outclassed, you are,
You've got to think high to rise,
You've got to be sure of yourself before
You can ever win a prize.
"Life's battles don't always go
To the stronger or faster man,
But soon or late the man who wins
Is the man who thinks he can!"*

Really, it all comes down to one choice. Will you lead life, or will you let life lead you? How do you create a future that does not yet exist? How real is this idea of control, that we can intentionally change the future for the better when there are so many unanswered questions in our minds? Is it possible to create a vision that is clear and real? That those questions fade away? Can our imagination be that powerful? Can we take an idea, a picture of the future, this intangible vision, and make it real? In fact, that's exactly the way it works. The world either unfolds around you, or it is shaped by people who see it differently.

# CHAPTER 4

## *Perseverance*

> *"The difference between a successful person and others is not a lack of strength, not a lack of knowledge, but rather a lack of will"*

Perseverance: in the dictionary, it means to do something despite struggle or delay, to achieve your personal goals. Personally, looking at all these success stories and engaging with Mr Cox I believe perseverance is much more than that. I don't disagree with the definition. But there is always more to a word. I believe perseverance is going to places you have never been yet, where others won't ever go. Perseverance is fighting when others don't have the courage too, so they just end up letting go. What is perseverance to you? What have you gone through? Who told you to stop? Were they over the top? How did you respond? Were you a big frog in a little pond? Or were you a little frog in a big pond? What went through your head when I asked you these questions? Now think of a time when you were extremely happy. And you thought nothing could go wrong? And that one thing that could bring you down, did. But then you improvised life, that's perseverance.

There is a great power of perseverance. Any worthwhile goal in your life is most likely going to take a tonne of this rare attribute. Though that might sound pretty obvious to most, very few actually lack the real perseverance needed to make big goals turn into reality. Chasing dreams and listing big time life changing goals seems pretty fun while putting it on paper. But any seasoned dreamer will tell you that the amount of time and energy required to make them actually happen is often stacked miles higher than they had originally anticipated. When most people reach these inevitable bridges along their journey they give up. Realizing things are much tougher than what they originally thought and decide to take an easier route. Bear in mind these are the ones who actually dare to chase their dreams in the first place. Many might criticize those who give up on their dreams but in all honesty, I can totally understand it. Of course, in this book I want to encourage people to go after their passion. But I cannot lie it is not easy, not by a long shot. I totally get why only a small percentage of people do succeed. But anyone who has made it to the other side will tell you that you need courage, imagination, and a load of persistence. This was a trait Mr Cox soon had to grasp on his journey. Previous experience taught Mr Cox that every level he has reached was always met by a new devil trying to hold him back from what he genuinely wanted.

After being sent back to Jamaica Mr Cox had only two choices. He could give up and blame the unfortunate events which left his dream crippled or accept what has happened, take responsibility and continue to chase his dream like his life depended on it. At first this was a question that Mr Cox was not mentally ready to answer.

Mr Cox started to isolate himself from the rest of the family, he hardly ever ate and the only time he went out was to go on top of the hill where his dream home was to be built. All that was there were building materials and a large hole in the ground where the foundation was set. Mr Cox closed his eyes, took a deep breath and imagined his home being completed. Tear drops started drizzling down his cheeks. He had made his mind up. He could not undo what happened, he could only learn from it. I can, I will, I must.

Success is good but failure is better. You must not let successes get to your head but also not let failure consume your heart. Know that, sometimes, actually most times, things do not go as planned and that is perfectly fine. For many individuals, it is simply easier to give up when things do not work out. But if there is one thing you should not do it is just that; do not give up because the reality is you are going to fail, a lot. But failure does not mean your idea was invalid or that your dream is not good enough. Failure means there is something to be learned or another direction to be taken. When defeat comes, accept it as a signal that your plans are not sound, rebuild those plans, and set sail once more toward your coveted goal. If you give up before your goal has been reached, you are a "quitter". A quitter never wins, and a winner never quits.

The struggle you're in today is developing the strength you need for tomorrow. If you fall a hundred times make sure you get up a hundred and one.

Mr Cox's mother was walking up the hill one day. She knew she'd find him standing in the same spot, staring into what should be the base of his dream home. She couldn't bear to see him be miserable anymore. She had to be honest to her first born "Son, your eagerness will indicate clearly how much or how little you really want to accumulate your goal. Fortunes gravitate to men whose minds have been prepared to attract it, just as surely as water gravitates to the ocean."

Mr Cox then had a definite decision he was to go back to the United Kingdom to finish off what he started. How? It did not matter to him. Mr Cox found life again. He looked upon the plot and pictured what his future home would look like. Two storey white house with a burgundy roof, with a staircase going up towards the top of the house leading to a platform where people can enjoy the view from the top of the hill. Six bedrooms, three en suites so that his future family can be comfortable. Large kitchen with marble floors, large dining room where the Sunday dinner will be taking place. Spacious front room for when you're feeling lazy. A garage that can hold a half a dozen cars, all walls painted clean white. This dream was not going to build itself. No one was going to build this dream home either. And sitting at home, miserable, placing blame on the world, wasn't going to help.

Poverty is attracted to the one whose mind is favourable to it, as money is attracted to him whose mind has been deliberately prepared to attract it, and through the same laws. Poverty consciousness will voluntarily seize the mind which is not occupied with the money consciousness. A poverty consciousness develops without conscious application of habits favourable to it. The money consciousness must be created, unless one is born with such a consciousness.

As long as you have hard work in your stride, good luck will always be by your side. This is what came Mr Cox's way. After finding his motivation back and the will to make do on his dream, he switched on his mobile phone to begin arranging plans for his return back to the United Kingdom. Previously ashamed of getting himself into his current position he was afraid of contacting his partner Jane. He felt like he let her down tremendously. The first person on the list for Mr Cox to call was Jane. Not for help. But just to apologise for leaving her in the dark. They spoke for hours on the phone, Mr Cox reassured her everything was going to be alright and he would be right back by her side. She said she knew, "But there'll be company." Mr Cox didn't follow on at first. "I'm pregnant." Mr Cox was stunned. "Now I need you here with me." Still stunned, then full of joy, Mr cox assured his partner he'd be there less than a week. Mr Cox proceeded to call Mr Patel, the taxi company owner. He explained to Mr Patel the situation. Mr Patel already knew what happened, and he knew about the deportation. As the immigration office came down hard with him on fines and legal wrongdoing. Mr Cox then asked to send all the money he had saved from acquiring drivers. "That money was used to pay for the fines you caused." Mr Cox was never an argumentative man. He always believed every person you come in contact with has a valuable lesson to teach you. Mr Patel and Mr Cox joint ventures had come to end. Mr Cox was back at square one.

Mr Cox did have some money put aside which he left with Jane. The crops were doing enough to keep the family back home afloat. This meant the dream had to be put on hold. But Mr Cox believed everything would work out to plan. Plus, he had a deadline when the house was to be finished. He commenced the building of the house to still be continued. He left the eldest of the brothers to watch over the development.

Mr Cox's siblings all wanted to come with him back to London. His two younger sisters both knew what they'll do as careers once they finished their studying. Also, the younger brother would love to go to England as well. He also had his eyes set at what he wanted to do. The baby brother had no fantasy of ever leaving his mother and father alone. Mr Cox was about to have a family of his own and found out his family also wanted a shot to grow in the city. Mr Cox's siblings became dreamers. He realised how important his actions were and now he was leading by example. Failure was never an option.

Those who cultivate the habit of persistence seem to benefit from an insurance against failure. No matter how many times they are defeated, they eventually arrive at the top of the ladder. Sometimes it appears that there is a hidden guide whose duty is to test people through all sorts of discouraging experiences. Those who pick themselves up after defeat and keep on trying, arrive. The world cries, "Bravo! I knew you could do it!" The hidden guide lets no one enjoy great achievement without passing the persistence test. Those who can't take it, simply do not make the grade. Those who can are bountifully rewarded for their persistence. They receive, as their compensation, whatever goal they are pursuing. That is not all! They receive something infinitely more important than material compensation – the knowledge that "every failure brings with it the seed of an equivalent advantage."

Soon upon arriving back to the London Heathrow airport, Mr Cox was greeted by Jane. Jane had figured out a way she could get Mr Cox stay in the United Kingdom indefinite. It was getting married. They were both fond of the idea. They loved each other and they both knew they would have been married eventually, they just didn't expect it to happen under these circumstances, but the pair was beaming at the idea. This was also a perfect opportunity for his younger brother and younger sisters to come up and experience London for themselves.

A baby on the way, a wedding to plan and a dream home currently undergoing construction.

Mr Cox remembered being introduced to an old small-time businessman. He was in the freight forwarding trade. He admired Mr Cox's work ethic, enthusiasm and charisma. The old timer was getting on in his years and he had no son or reliable hand to pass down his work to. Mr Cox went to see this man. He already had a worker, but this guy was lazy and incompetent. Mr Cox offered the man peace of mind. Mr Cox's proposition was, "You show me the ropes and I can offer you peace of mind and I will never let you down."

When it came knocking, did you hear it? When it was in front of you, did you see it? Or did you look right through it? Completely oblivious to what you had. Opportunity is a subtle creature. A mystery to the universe. Misinterpreted as an obvious treasure calling out to you. When in actuality it's the map. It's the road. It's the courage to move forward. Opportunity is not the moon, the sun or the stars. It's the staircase that takes you higher. The pieces that comes together to comprise your universe. And when that sun comes up let the light set your eyes open. You wake up and breathe your first breath. Understand that you are breathing in opportunity. It's not what you look at. It's what you see and benefit from the message. It's easy to push this away as insignificant or fluff. But let me ask you this. How does one person turn adversity into the very reason they succeed, and another turn that same adversity into a ball and chain? Why do some run toward chaos and others retreat? How can one person transform a loss now into a win later and another person views that same defeat as the end? Well, the answer is simple, really. Did you seek out the opportunity, or did you not? That is the question. When you strip life down of its complexities the patterns become apparent. The people who win never ask if it's possible. If it can happen. No, they begin with the premise that it sure can. The question is how. How can I make this a reality? How can I turn the world around me? The events taking place, whether challenging, strenuous, reassuring or anything in between. How can I position them to lift me up? That is the opportunity. Without that realization there never will be your pot of gold. It begins in your head and is projected out. They say, "Fake it till you make it." There's something to that because if you never put a dream, or a goal or a plan into existence, no matter how small, it simply fails to exist. You have to see your city on the hill. When it's just rocks. It's not a waste, it's not stupid, it's not irrational because you know what it can be. They don't, but you do and that's opportunity. Their wasteland is your future empire. Their hopelessness is your reassurance. They see blank space. And you see infinity waiting to be unpacked and expanded. There will be a day when they'll wonder how you did it, how you made what you have a reality. You saw it. You simply saw what could be and when you see opportunity your mind, your body and your life conform. Throw away the ifs and start asking how. In your work there are no problems, just opportunities. In your world there are no ends. Just new beginnings.

The freight forwarding trade was a dirty business, a lot of young men weren't interested in driving round in lorries all day. Breaking their backs carrying large goods around in filthy overalls. Working all hours of the night. Mr Cox was prone to hard work, but all his efforts were temporary; he now wanted something that would last and that could grow bigger than him.

There is no substitute for persistence! It cannot be supplanted by any other quality! Remember this, and it will hearten you, in the beginning, when the going may seem difficult and slow.

# CHAPTER 5

## *Vision*

Imagination is everything. It is the preview of life's coming attractions.

Many years ago, I read what Napoleon Hill pointed out: imagination is the most marvellous, miraculous, inconceivably powerful force that the world has ever known. The average individual uses the imagination "if they use it at all" against themselves. They imagine what they don't want. They imagine the problems coming. Let's begin to use our imagination the way God/Universe intended it to be used. It's the greatest creative faculty that we possess. And we can build anything we want with it.

I want you to wonder around your home or possibly your office. And take a look at all of the conveniences that you have there. That you didn't have, let's say, two, five, ten, twenty years ago. Did you know that everything without exception was created in the mind of one individual with their imagination? You can use your imagination to go into the future and bring it into the present. That's what all phenomenally successful people do. They see where they want to go and then they act like the person they want to become.

Albert Einstein – "Imagination is more important than knowledge. For knowledge is limited to all we now know and understand, while imagination embraces the entire world, and all there ever will be to know and understand."

After being sent back to Jamaica, Mr Cox had a vision that the next time he was to step foot on British soil. He would build something for himself. His first dream of his white mansion that was built on top of the hill, viewing the whole of the island below him. He saw his parents, siblings, family and friends being taken care of thanks to the result of his hard work.

Ideas are the beginning points of all fortunes. Ideas are products of imagination. Generally speaking, an idea is an impulse of thought that impels action by an appeal to imagination. Millions of people go through life hoping for favourable "breaks". Perhaps a favourable break can get one an opportunity, but the plan is not to depend upon luck.

Mr Cox had an idea. An idea that could go two ways. It could fail or it could be successful. His future and his family's life were too important for him to even think about failure. His mind was focused on what he wanted. Mr Cox believed that it was possible. Nothing to lose but everything to gain. Even if you were to crash and burn the experience itself would be worth ten times the cost.

When Mr Cox was on the roads, picking up and dropping off, picking up and dropping off, passenger after passenger, picking up and dropping off, although for some this may seem a daunting experience for Mr Cox was a learning curve. He learnt from everyone he came in contact with. He started to see a pattern in people's moods and behaviour. The wealthy were more relaxed and when they had an issue, they worked on resolving that issue. But the poor – and when I say poor, I don't mean the way the person dressed, or the money they had in the bank, but poor thinking – they only focused on their problems and not on how to solve them.

The freight forwarding business to the Caribbean Islands for importing and exporting for personal uses and small businesses was a niche business at the time. The old timers that were currently in the trade were sick of the back breaking hard labour work. They wanted to sit back. Every time they manage to bring a potential replacement. It would go either two ways. The apprentice would not be cut out for the work or the potential candidate would take off with the money, as the majority of times the customers were paying cash in hand at the time. The old timers lacked trust and were focusing on the problem at hand instead of thinking of a solution. This is where Mr Cox came in. There were four freight forwarding companies in London in the early 90s who specialised in importing and exporting to the Caribbean. Each individual had similar things in common. They were all getting on in age. Their methods were outdated. Mr Cox did his homework. All parties had a viable business that actually could prosper, if Mr Cox could unite the four and propose his idea for the future. Mr Cox planned to ensure the gentlemen. Reduce ongoing business expenses. Ramp up the productivity in the business. Create an easier new customer service process. Increase traffic to the business and improve financial wealth.

Ideas are intangible forces, but they have more power than the physical brains that give birth to them. They have the power to live on, after the brain that gave birth to them. They have the power to live on, after the brain that creates them has returned to dust. For example, take the power of Christianity. That began with a simple idea, born in the brain of Christ. Its chief tenet was, "Do unto others as you would have others do unto you." Christ has gone back to the source from whence He came, but His ideas still go marching on.

Have you ever asked yourself, "Why do we think we have to work hard if we're going to win? It takes hard work! Years of hard work!" That isn't good information, in fact it's a lie. Stop and think for a minute of the people who you know are working really hard. For a long time. And they're not winning at all. They are broke. They are renting a place to live. They don't own their own home. Probably driving a used car. The idea of working hard is silly. In Think and Grow

Rich, Napoleon Hill writes there are thirty major causes of failures that I'll list below. There are thirteen principles to success that I'll also list below. He said that if you're one of those people who believe that hard work and honesty alone will bring riches, you should suppress that thought because it is not true. Riches when they come in huge quantities are never the result of hard work. Riches come, if they come at all, in response to definite demands based upon the application of definite principles and not by chance or luck.

Paper is formed into what we call money. Money is an idea. Money goes where it is invited and stays where it's welcomed. The idea you have to work hard for this stuff, it's not true. Some of the people who work the hardest, earn the least. Think about it. I was reading Taylor Swift, a young, female singer. Was the highest paid entertainer in two thousand and eighteen. She is doing what she absolutely loves. That's not hard work. When you love what you are doing, you'll never work again. See, I see work as something you don't enjoy, and you don't want to do and drains a lot of energy. Napoleon Hill spent his entire life studying five hundred of the world's most successful people. He became imminent friends with people like Henry Ford, Thomas Edison, Harvey Firestone. They were doing what they absolutely loved. They changed the whole world. Ford put us on wheels, Edison illuminated the place. They were doing what they loved, and they earned millions. What do you love doing?

The thirty major causes of failure. This is straight from Napoleon Hill's *Think and Grow Rich.*

How many of these are holding you back?

1. Unfavourable hereditary background. There is but little, if anything, which can be done for people who are born with a deficiency in brain power. This philosophy offers but one method of bridging the weakness – through the aid of the master mind. Observe with

profit, however, that this is the only one of thirty causes of failure which may not be easily corrected by any individual.
2. Lack of a well-defined purpose in life. There is no hope of success for the person who does not have a central purpose, or a definite goal at which to aim. Ninety-eight out of every hundred of those whom Napoleon Hill has analysed, had no such aim. Perhaps this was the major cause of their failure.
3. Lack of ambition to aim above mediocrity. We offer no hope for the person who is so indifferent as not to want to get ahead in life, and who is not willing to pay the price.
4. Insufficient education. This is a handicap which may be overcome with comparative ease. Experience has proven that the best-educated people are often those who are known as self-made, or self-educated. It makes more than a college degree to make one a person of education. Any person who is educated is one who has learned to get whatever he wants in life without violating the rights of others. Education consists, not so much of knowledge, but of knowledge effectively and persistently applied. Men are paid not merely for what they know, but more particularly for what they do with what they know.
5. Lack of self-discipline. Discipline comes through self-control. This means that one must control all negative qualities. Before you can control conditions, you must first control yourself. Self-mastery is the hardest job you will ever tackle. If you do not conquer self, you will be conquered by self. You may see at one and the same time both your best friend and your greatest enemy, by stepping in front of a mirror.
6. Ill health. No person may enjoy outstanding success

without good health. Many of the causes of ill health are subject to mastery and control. These, in the main are:
- a. Overeating unhealthy foods.
- b. Wrong habits of thought; giving expression to negatives.
- c. Wrong use of and overindulgence in sex.
- d. Lack of proper physical exercise.
- e. An inadequate supply of fresh air, due to improper breathing.

7. Unfavourable environmental influences during childhood. "As the twig is bent, so shall the tree grow." Most people who have criminal tendencies acquire them as the result of bad environments, and improper associates during childhood.
8. Procrastination. This is one of the most common causes of failure. "Old man procrastination" stands within the shadow of every human being, waiting for his opportunity to spoil one's chances of success. Most of us go through life as failures. Because we are waiting for the "time to be right." Start where you stand, and work with whatever tools you may have at your command, and better tools will be found as you go along.
9. Lack of persistence. Most of us are good "starters" but poor "finishers" of everything we begin. Moreover, people are prone to give up at first signs of defeat. There is no substitute for persistence. The person who makes persistence his watchword, discovers that "old man failure" finally becomes tired, and makes his departure. Failure cannot cope with persistence.
10. Negative personality. There is no hope of success for the person who repels people through a negative personality. Success comes through the application of power, and power is attained through the cooperative

efforts of other people. A negative personality will not induce cooperation.

11. Lack of controlled sexual urge. Sex energy is the most powerful of all the stimuli which move people into action. Because it is the most powerful of the emotions, it must be controlled, through transmutation, and converted into other channels.

12. Uncontrolled desire for "something for nothing." The gambling instinct drives millions of people to failure. Evidence of this may be found in a study of the Wall Street crash of '29, during which millions of people tried to make money by gambling on stock margins.

13. Lack of well-defined power of decision. Men who succeed reach decisions promptly, and change them, if it all, very slowly, and change them frequently, and quickly. Indecision and procrastination are twin brothers. Where one is found, the other may usually be found also. Kill off this pair before they completely "hog-tie" you to the treadmill of failure.

14. One or more of the six basic fears
    - The fear of poverty
    - The fear of criticism
    - The fear of ill health
    - The fear of losing someone's love
    - The fear of old age
    - The fear of death

15. Wrong selection of a mate in marriage. This is the most common cause of failure. Marriage connects people intimately, and unless this relationship is harmonious, failure is likely to follow. Moreover, it will be a form of failure that is marked by misery and unhappiness, destroying all signs of ambition.

16. Over-caution. The person who takes no chances, generally has to take whatever is left when others

are through choosing. Over-caution is as bad as under-caution. Both are extremes to be guarded against. Life itself is filled with the element of chance.

17. Wrong selection of associates in business. This is one of the most common causes of failure in business. In marketing personal services, one should use great care to select an employer who will be an inspiration, and who is, himself, intelligent and successful. We emulate those with whom we associate most closely. Pick an employer who is worth emulating.
18. Superstition and prejudice. Superstition is a form of fear. It is also a sign of ignorance. Men who succeed keep open minds and are afraid of nothing.
19. Wrong selection of a vocation. No man can succeed in a line of endeavour which he does not like. The most essential step in the marketing of personal services is that of selecting an occupation into which you can throw yourself wholeheartedly.
20. Lack of concentration of effort. The "jack-of-all-trades" seldom is good at any. Concentrate all of your efforts on one definite chief aim.
21. The habit of indiscriminate spending. The spendthrift cannot succeed, mainly because he stands eternally in fear of poverty. Form the habit of systematic saving by putting aside a definite percentage of your income. Money in the bank gives one a very safe foundation of courage when bargaining for the sale of personal services. Without money, one must take what one is offered, and be glad to get it.
22. Lack of enthusiasm. Without enthusiasm one cannot be convincing. Moreover, enthusiasm is contagious, and the person who has it under control is generally welcome in any group of people.
23. Intolerance. The person with a "closed" mind on any

subject seldom gets ahead. Intolerance means that one has stopped acquiring knowledge. The most damaging forms of intolerance are those connected with religious, racial, and political differences of opinion.

24. Intemperance. The most damaging forms of intemperance are connected with eating, strong drink, and sexual activities. Over-indulgence in any of these is fatal to success.
25. Inability to cooperate with others. More people lose their positions and their big opportunities in life, because of this fault, than for all other reasons combined. It is a fault which no well-informed businessman, or leader will tolerate.
26. Possession of power that was not acquired though self-effort. (Daughters and sons of wealthy men, and others who inherit money which they did not earn.) Power in the hands of one who did acquire it gradually, is often fatal to success. Quick riches are more dangerous than poverty.
27. International dishonesty. There is no substitute for honesty. One may be temporarily dishonest by force of circumstance over which one has no control, without permanent damage. But there is no hope for the person who is dishonest by choice. Sooner or later, his deeds will catch up with him, and he will pay by loss of reputation, and perhaps even loss of liberty.
28. Egotism and vanity. These qualities serve as red lights which warn others to keep away. They are fatal to success.
29. Guessing instead of thinking. Most people are too indifferent or lazy to acquire facts with which to think accurately. They prefer to act on "opinions" created by guesswork or snap-judgements.
30. Lack of capital. This is a common cause of failure

among those who start out in business for the first time, without sufficient reserve of capital to absorb the shock of their mistakes, and to carry them over until they have established a reputation.

In these thirty major causes of failure is found a description of the tragedy of life, which obtains for practically every person who tries and fails. It will be helpful if you can induce someone who knows you well to go over this list with you and help you analyse your behaviour by the standards of the thirty causes of failure. It may be beneficial if you try this alone. Most people cannot see themselves as others see them, you may be one who cannot.

It's not a matter of whether or not we can. Everybody can, but not everybody will. How to turn nothing into something? How tangible are ideas? And imagination? Ideas that become so powerful in your mind and your consciousness that they seem surreal to you, even before they become tangible. Imagination that is so strong you could actually see it. If somebody cannot see it when it is not here, then it will never be here. Then it will never be here. Start looking into the future of what you like to accomplish. Where you would like to go, the person you would like to become. Decide what you want. And then act as if you already have it. That is to believe that what you imagined is possible for you.

The first step is to imagine what's possible. The second step is to believe. Here is the third step. And that is to go to work and make it real. You now go to work and make it a movement, you make it tangible, you make it viable. You breathe life into it and then you construct it.

You and only you are the subject that impacts the burning desire in your imagination.

# CHAPTER 6

## *Manifestation*

*"Expect to manifest everything that you want to manifest."*

We all have a multitude of thoughts and desires swirling around inside of us competing for attention and dominance. Your desires can involve every area of your life. Maybe you want to focus more on your health. Or your wealth, your career, relationships or your physical self or spiritual self. Whatever the case may be, the trick to attention setting is to fully involve yourself and make things happen. Without investing your self-worth or emotional well-being into their manifestation. Imagine there are two separate elements involved in creating anything you want into the physical reality. Number one is the mental and the physical participation. This is the extent in which someone put their creative and physical energy into the creation to a specific outcome. And number two is emotional participation. This is to the extent in which a person puts their happiness, self-worth and well-being on the line in the pursuit to a specific outcome.

Quantum physics tells us that when energy is entwined with the consciousness, we pull from an infinite number of possibilities that are available to us and manifest in our physical reality. We are partly a product of our environment and the experiences we've had in our formative years; we had the ability to alter any portion of our surroundings and create a new future. Once we understand how and why the power of our minds is so crucial in doing so, we live in two simultaneous worlds. The invisible world of cause where thoughts and beliefs are creators and the seemingly material world of affect where the results or manifestations of thoughts or beliefs come into being and are experienced. The law of creation is exact and easily demonstrated through the invisible idea of a plant with a seed. That idea is within the seed before it was even planted. And that seed would produce only the particular plant which is invisible within it. Both physical scientists and metaphysicians agree that the physical world is a constant change. The more we learn about the inner or invisible world in which humans exist, we realise that this invisible world is infinite. Humankind, who is in the image and likeness of the infinite intelligent power, is also infinite and has available to him and her an ever-expanding intelligence.

Through the law of creation humanity can project an idea into the mind and have that idea come into manifestation. With this knowledge we can take control, start to shape our life and reality from a creative consciousness paradigm. Once fully understood, we can shed ourselves of our old paradigms reality that can strain us. And accelerate the ushering in of a new reality which empowers and creates a basis of total wellness. We must take our own unfoldment in our hands and give conscious direction to the evolutionary forces within us. From the perspective of quantum physics the universe is made up entirely of energy. Science also states all things are interconnected, interdependent, and essentially one or unified.

All of us have within us the amazing capacity to manifest and attract anything that we want into our lives.

Born and raised on a farm to a poverty-stricken family. With no money, just food from the land to live off. Always grateful that his parents were able to feed him and his siblings. Having to walk miles to and from school with his bare feet, only to be denied continuing with his studies. Forced to work on the farm with his father, just like his father before him was.

Everything that comes to you in terms of manifestation. Now what's manifestation? Is it a car? Sure! Is the house you live in or the house that's on the way to you? Yes, that manifestation. Is it your empire, is it your work, is it the people who surround you? Yes, and yes. Manifestation is all of that, but I want you to begin to realize or feel that what manifestation is or what we are talking about is what is happening to you now. In other words, you reading this book is manifestation right now. Everything that you're doing moment by moment is a manifestation.

When you discover this creative power within yourself, you will boldly assert the supremacy of imagination and put all things in subjection to it. When we speak of God, are we totally unaware that this power called God is in our imagination? This is the creative power in us. There is nothing underneath the sky that is not plastic as pottery clay to the touch of shaping the spirit of imagination.

I want to show you today how to put your wonderful imagination right into the feeling of your wish fulfilled. Remain in the state of your wish fulfilled and I promise you from my own experience you will realise the state in which you sleep. If you can actually feel yourself right into the situation of your fulfilled desire and continue therein until you fall asleep. Remain in it until you give it all the tonnes of reality, until you give it all the sensory vividness of reality. As you do it, in that state, quietly fall away into sleep and dim away. You will consciously devise a means that will employ you to move across a series of events leading you towards the objective realisation of this state. Now here is a practical technique. The first thing you do, you must know exactly what you want in this world. When you know exactly what you want, make as lifelike a representation as possible. On what you would see, and what you would touch, and what you would do when physically moving in such a state. For example, suppose I wanted a home, but I had no money. But I still know what I want. Without taking anything else into consideration, I would make a lifelike representation of the home that I want, with all the things in it that I want. Then, at night, as I am going to bed, I would imagine, in a state of drowsiness, that I am actually in that house. I would imagine that, were I to step off the bed, I would step upon the floor of that house. Was I to leave the room, I would enter the adjacent room in that house. While I am touching the furniture and feeling it to be solidly real and while I am moving from one room to the other in my imaginary house, I fall asleep in that state and I know that, in a way I cannot consciously devise, I would realise my house. Was I to leave this room I would enter the that is adjacent to my imagines room in that house and while I am touching the furniture and feeling it to be solidly real and while I am moving from one room to the other in my imaginary house I would go sound asleep in that state and I know that in a way I could not consciously devise I would realise my house. I have seen it work time and time again. If I wanted a promotion in my business, I would ask myself what additional responsibilities would I have if I were to be given this great promotion. What would I do, what would I say, what would I see, how would I act? And then, in my imagination, I would begin to see, and touch, and act, and I would ultimately see, and touch, and act as if I was in that position. People are totally unaware of this fantastic power of the imagination. But when we discover this power within, we never play the part that we formerly played. We don't turn back and become just reflective on life, from here on in we are the effect of life. The secret of it is to centre your imagination in the feeling of the wish fulfilled and remain there.

Enjoy the journey not the destination. A lot of us delay our

Happiness. " I will be happy when I get to this level, when I get my degree, when I get my dream job, when I get married, when I have kids." Instead, enjoy the journey. Enjoy the whole process, everyday. Enjoy that you get up to strive for whatever you're after.

Many people have this idea that they want to achieve something great or be somebody great. And they neglect the step that leads to greatness. They don't honour this step at this moment because they have this idea of some future moment when they're going to be great. Life is a journey; you're going to go from here to there. Whenever you are going to get there nobody knows, and maybe on the way you'll branch out to somewhere else, but at least you have a certain direction. It's good to have some direction in your life. But while you are travelling, if your destination takes up most of your attention and you are continuously focusing on the outcome, you really can't enjoy the journey, and most of your life is the journey. The arrival is relatively rare. Your whole life consists of the steps you are taking at this moment. There is never anything else.

Nearly two years had gone by. Mr Cox had welcomed his first-born son from his now wife Jane Cox. It was ninety ninety-three. The universe was answering to all Mr Cox wanted and desired. The shell of his dream home was completed, and Mr Cox needed to go back to Jamaica to start the preparations of the inside of his future home. At the back of Mr Cox's mind, he remembered a promise he had made to his siblings. A promise to bring them to the United Kingdom for them to pursue a dream of their own. Mr Cox was one of four partners in the newly formed business. Business was thriving month to month. In the moment Mr Cox thought if he could sell his share of the business, he could then be independent to run off on his ventures whilst also being able to fulfil his promise to his brothers and sisters.

When Mr Cox arrived in Jamaica with his wife Jane and his son Jamaal, his mother and father and friends and family greeted his family with heaps of praises. Mr Cox was the first person in his whole district to have gone from pillar to post seeking out a better life for his future and for his loved ones. With the fruits that Mr Cox bared along his journey, he provided work for the local builder in his area. He provided raw materials so that the locals could grow more fruits and vegetables they could sell. Mr Cox couldn't imagine that along his journey he would be helping so many others. Once Mr Cox finally got settled, the family gathered around for dinner. He had another surprise. He had arranged for his younger brother and two younger sisters an opportunity to come over to London. The youngest of Mr Cox's brothers wanted to stay, his heart was in Jamaica and he wanted to stay with his mother and father. The other three siblings couldn't believe what their older brother had just said to them. Tears of joy came to each of their eyes.

The first week Mr Cox was taking his wife and son around Jamaica, showing Jane where it all started, where he had to walk to school in his bare feet every morning and every evening. Showing his family, the beauty in the island. Mr Cox then had daily visits with the builders and interior designers instructing them on every detail of how he wanted his home to look on the inside. Mr Cox was approached by his younger brother and he said to him, "You did it. Now, what do you plan to do now?" Mr Cox replied, "Enjoy and learn from each moment. You know I never got to stay in school like everyone else. I thought I was missing out on learning. But life itself has been my teacher and I'm going to continue learning from life."

If you want to live an amazing life, a truly abundant happy life, make it a priority to live more in the present moment. You don't need fancy cars, you don't millions of pounds or dollars, you don't need things. All you need is what's within you now. All you need is this very moment, right now. This precious present moment. To be part of all the miracles that are around you and indeed a part of you right now. All unhappiness is formed when we take our being away from the present moment. Stress, disappointment and anger, or when we think about events of our past that we have no control over right now. Anxiety or worry when we think about the future also which we have no control over right now. Most of us seem to be always searching for someplace else, some better moment in the future but that moment never comes. Because when that moment comes, we want more. We should just stop and appreciate everything there is in this moment. Everything we take for granted. Like the life in our bodies, like the energy inside us, like the miracle of human life, like the miracle of creation, the wonder of this universe, the wonder of you being able to communicate with all parts of your body without speaking a word. The wonder of our sentences, the sun, the rain, the air you breathe in right now. And when we can truly grasp this powerful present moment there are no problems. They are only miracles. Many thinks being lost in the present moment might eliminate any chance of growth or success in their life however the opposite is true. When everything you do is infused with your presence, everything you do is done with more quality, more connection, with more love and when you are more connected with everything you do, there is greater success on all levels. The success that all of us seek is really just the feeling we believe we will get in achieving it. Therefore, the success itself is really a feeling and any feeling even the highest elation can be achieved right now. When your attention and your appreciation is one hundred percent focused on this perfect present moment. When we stop seeking an end point and instead make each moment an end in itself.

When we can appreciate the journey so much that a destination is not needed. The journey is the new destination, new miracle. That's what life is really all about. Making the most out of each moment, appreciating the wonder and the miracles of each moment. You need nothing materially speaking. You are complete as you are, right now.

# CHAPTER 7

## *Universal Law*

If you want to find the secrets of the universe, think in terms of energy, frequency and vibration. The universe responds to our inner yearnings by mysteriously bringing people into our life to answer our questions and help quell our conflicts. Every time you follow your intuition, your personal vibration intensifies. This can be likened to turning up the volume on a stereo. The more your personal vibration is intensified the more you will pull people into your life who carry messages for you. It is a universal law.

There are fourteen universal laws that I believe govern life on earth. They say if you master these laws, you will have mastered life on the physical level. Nothing on earth happens unless through these laws. Each law is interconnected and intertwined with the next.

One, the law of divine oneness. The first out of the fourteen universal laws help us to understand that we live in a world where everything is connected to everything else. All is energy and all energy is an extension of source energy. Everything we do, say, think and believe affects others in the universe around us. We are microcosms of the macrocosm. We are all parts of the same source.

Two, the law of vibration. This law states that everything in the universe moves, vibrates and travels in a circular pattern. The same principles of vibration in the physical world apply to our thoughts, feelings, desires, and wills in the etheric world. Each sound, word, object and even thought has its own vibrational frequency unique unto itself.

Three, the law of action. The law of action must be applied in order for us to manifest things on earth. Therefore, we must engage in actions that support our thoughts, dreams, emotions, and words. Action is energy in motion.

Four, the law of correspondence. This law states that the principles or laws of physics that explain the physical world, energy, light, vibration and motion have their corresponding principles in the spiritual world. What happens on the inside will reflect on the outside. If you are hectic and stressed, your world will also be. If you are in total bliss, the outside world will then mirror that bliss. "As above, so below. As within, so without."

Five, the law of cause and effect. The universal law states that nothing happens by chance or outside the universal laws. Every action has a reaction or consequence. If I am thinking successful thoughts, speaking like I am already successful, feeling like a success and taking successful actions. The end result will have to be success. We reap what we have sown.

Six, the law of compensation. This law is the law of cause and effect applied to blessings and abundance that are provided for us. The visible effects of our deeds are given to us in gifts, money, inheritances, friendships and blessings. The good that we do eventually comes back to us in different forms matching the same energy. If you want to increase your compensation you must increase the value of your contribution. Do more of what you have been asked and you will be compensated abundantly.

Seven, the law of attraction. This law demonstrates how we attract the objects, events and people that come into our lives. Our thoughts, feelings, words and actions produce energies which in turn attract like energies. Negative energies attract negative energies and positive energies attract positive energies.

Eight, the law of perpetual transmutation of energy. This

eighth law out of the fourteen universal laws is a powerful one. It states that all persons have within them the power to change the conditions in their lives. Higher vibration consumes and transforms lower ones thus each of us can change the energies in our lives by understanding the universal laws and applying the principles in such a way as to effect change. At any time, you can switch vibrations from negative to positive. You can always change your conditions; you are never stuck.

Nine, the law of gestation. The law of gestation, also called the law of divine timing, states that everything has its gestational period or time to manifest. Every thought, word, feeling and action is a seed. Once nourished with enough focus and energy that seed germinates into life's situations and circumstances. Your desires, goals and innermost thoughts will manifest in divine timing and not a moment sooner.

Ten, the law of relativity. This law states that each person will receive a series of challenges, tests of initiation for the purpose of strengthening the light within. We must consider each of these tests to be an opportunity and remain connected to our hearts when proceeding to solve the problems. This law also teaches us to compare our problems to other problems and put everything into its proper perspective. No matter how bad we perceive our situation to be there is always someone who is in a worse position. It is all relative, it is all perspective.

Eleven, the law of polarity. This law states that everything is on a continuum and has an opposite. There cannot be hot without cold. There cannot be up without down. There cannot be extreme negative without extreme positive. We can suppress and disperse negative thoughts and energy by concentrating on its opposite. If you are negative we can always switch our vibration to attract positive energy by focusing on the positive. What we focus on expands in our reality.

Twelve, the law of rhythm, this law states that everything vibrates and moves to a certain rhythm. These rhythms establish seasons, cycles, stages of developments and patterns. Life is a series of ebb and flow. The tide goes out and goes back in again. Each cycle reflects the regularity of the source universe. Masters know how to rise above negative or challenging seasons by never getting too excited or allowing negative things to penetrate their consciousness. They focus solely on what they want and so their reality reflects just that.

Thirteen, the law of belief. This law states that whatever we fully believe with thought, emotion and conviction eventually becomes our reality. We are always creating laws for ourselves based on what we believe to be true. Even if a thing isn't factually true. Our belief will make it so.

Fourteen, the law of gender. This last law out of the fourteen universal laws states that everything is masculine (yang) and feminine (yin) principles. And that these are the basis for all creation. The spiritual initiate must balance the masculine and feminine energies within herself or himself to become a master and a true co-creator with source.

Master these laws and you will become a master manifester and a deliberate co-creator of the physical world.

## *Index*

| | |
|---|---|
| 9 | Introduction |
| 14 | Chapter 1. Want |
| 26 | Chapter 2. State of Mind |
| 38 | Chapter 3. Belief |
| 54 | Chapter 4. Perseverance |
| 62 | Chapter 5. Vision |
| 72 | Chapter 6. Manifestation |
| 80 | Chapter 7. Universal Law |

europe books